Understanding the United States Debt

Tyler L. Chessman

www.UnderstandingTheUSDebt.com

www.UnderstandingTheUSDebt.com

Cover design by Ana Grigoriu

Printed in the United States of America

BISAC: Business & Economics / Economics / General

ISBN-13: 978-1453835760
ISBN-10: 1453835768

"No pecuniary consideration is more urgent than the regular redemption and discharge of the public debt; on none can delay be more injurious, or an economy of time more valuable."
– George Washington

Table of Contents

Introduction

—

When in the Course of human events, it becomes necessary for one people to dissolve the political bands which have connected them with another, and to assume among the powers of the earth, the separate and equal station to which the Laws of Nature and of Nature's God entitle them, a decent respect to the opinions of mankind requires that they should declare the causes which impel them to the separation. – U.S. Declaration of Independence

In the Declaration of Independence, the American Colonies presented a case to justify their separation from England. One of their arguments revolved around Man's unalienable right to liberty, which their King had violated,

> *Such has been the patient sufferance of these Colonies; and such is now the necessity which constrains them to alter their former Systems of Government. The history of the present King of Great Britain is a history of repeated injuries and usurpations, all having in direct object the establishment of an absolute Tyranny over these States.*

The States won their freedom, and the United States of America became the most powerful and wealthy country in the world. With a form of government unlike anything else in Europe, the American citizen was given Life, Liberty, and the pursuit of Happiness. Life was protected, Liberty was assured, and Happiness was left to the individual.

In the 21st century, liberty in the U.S. is under attack. It is an attack from within, by those who believe Life is expendable, Liberty is unnecessary, and Happiness must be regulated. Consider a few of the charges levied against the King in the Declaration of Independence and ask yourself if the same could be said of the current government,

> *He has erected a multitude of New Offices, and sent hither swarms of Officers to harass [sic] our people, and eat out their substance*
> *For imposing Taxes on us without our Consent*
> *For taking away our Charters, abolishing our most valuable Laws, and altering fundamentally the Forms of our Governments*

A side effect of this attack is a massive amount of debt. In the early 1900's, the entire U.S. debt could have been paid off by the richest man in the world. In 2010, the four richest men in the world couldn't pay a year of the United States' interest payments. Benjamin Franklin knew the danger of debt,

Think what you do when you run in debt; you give to another the power over your liberty.

He also knew avoiding debt could occasionally require tough decisions,

Rather go to bed with out dinner than to rise in debt.

Over the long haul, governments, just like people, end up in debt due to decisions rather than circumstances. And as more decisions are taken away from the individual and given to the government, the more the debt of the country increases. From investing for retirement to providing health care or charity, the government cannot and will not operate as efficiently as the individual and the free market.

Debt is often the result of impatience, envy, and coveting; it is rarely the result of making too little money. That's a thought worth repeating, as people often talk about increasing income or taxes when it comes to dealing with debt. People don't like to talk about reducing spending.

Several years ago, I enjoyed listening to the Dave Ramsey show. Dave is a personal finance guru with a strong dislike of debt. People call into the show for financial advice; Dave rarely tells a listener that he or she has an income problem. Almost always, he tells them how to eliminate the sources of debt and the behaviors that led to the debt in the first place. Ultimately, we need to do the same thing at a national level. And, like Dave's typical advice, I believe we have a spending problem rather than an income problem.

In early 2009, I began hearing a daily and relentless warning call on the radio about the then "$11 trillion in debt! Trillion dollar deficits as far as the eye can see!"[1] Being an analytical person, I decided to do my own research. I am not an economist or a politician. In my day job, however, I help customers evaluate and use Business Intelligence software. I know how to combine, model, and analyze data. What I've learned makes me frightened, angry, and motivated to tell others.

Technical Notes

The information presented in this book comes from public sources. Where possible, the data was pulled directly from the government agency (e.g., the Bureau of Public Debt, the Bureau of Labor Statistics, etc.) responsible for collecting and producing a given data set. The charts and tables were created in Excel 2010. I used a new Excel add-in, called PowerPivot (www.powerpivot.com), to

- gather and store data from multiple sources
- create relationships among different data sets
- define custom calculations (e.g., last non-empty, yearly changes, etc.)
- analyze the data using Excel PivotTables and PivotCharts

An Excel workbook, which contains much of the data I present in this book, is available through the website www.UnderstandingTheUSDebt.com. If you want to dive further into a particular subject area, you'll need a copy of Office 2010 Professional (the PowerPivot add-in is free). I plan to post a brief tutorial for those who want to get more familiar with the data modeling and analysis techniques used in the workbook.

There is a good chance you'll find a number in my book that differs from a number you find elsewhere. Those who work in a large company know the challenges of trying to get to "one version of the truth" when analyzing business metrics like profitability, retention, or market share. Every organization I've worked with stores data across multiple systems. The data is often duplicated. Certain reports require extraction of data from multiple source systems in order to first transform and then harmonize the data. Some metrics may differ depending on the requestor – consider sales revenue. A financial analyst may want billed revenue. A sales manager may want revenue credited to his region. A services manager may only want to see revenue from service operations within a certain geographical area, which may or may not align with the sales manager's regional structure.

In this respect the U.S. government is similar to a large organization. Debt and economic data is stored across multiple agencies. Debt numbers are maintained by the U.S. Bureau of the Public Debt, an agency within the U.S. Treasury Department. Gross Domestic Product (GDP) is defined by the U.S. Department of Commerce Bureau of Economic Analysis (BEA). Government receipts and outlays are prepared by the Financial Management Service, part of the U.S. Treasury Department, though a comprehensive and download friendly historical summary is available from the Presidential Office of Management and Budget (OMB) or the U.S. Census Bureau. Data is sometimes changed or restated after it is initially reported. Some metrics have multiple definitions. For example, GDP is reported quarterly. The quarterly number is adjusted for the season and multiplied by 4 to produce a seasonally adjusted annual value[2]. GDP is also reported annually. The annual value is an average of its 4 quarterly values. So if I want to calculate debt as a percent of GDP for a given year, do I use the GDP for the last quarter or the annual average? Am I calculating debt as a percentage of GDP for a calendar year or a fiscal year? Is the calculation for the beginning of the year, or the end of the year?

I could go on, but the point is you will often find slight differences in calculations. In writing this book, I compared my numbers with other sources to look for glaring errors and to make sure there was a general consensus in calculations. So, if I tell you a given ratio is 83.62% and you find someone else saying it is 85.83%, don't be alarmed. Most of the numbers and trends in this book are so large that a small deviation makes little difference.

Acknowledgments

I give thanks to God for the blessings, patience, and forgiveness He has poured into my life. I also want to give a special thanks to my wife and mother-in-law for their help with editing and proofreading.

There are several radio talk show hosts who have warned about the national debt for years, and I give them credit for getting me interested in learning more about this topic. There are also organizations like the Heritage Foundation that provide well researched, clearly written, and free information that I referenced liberally in my book.

Chapter 1 – Overview and Historical Analysis

—

"I, however, place economy among the first and most important of republican virtues, and public debt as the greatest of the dangers to be feared." – Thomas Jefferson

Introduction

According to Webster's Collegiate Dictionary, debt is defined as "a state of owing" or "something owed: Obligation." Interestingly, it is also defined as "Sin, Trespass." All three definitions accurately describe the condition, history, and decisions leading to the persistent and rising debt of the U.S. federal government.

Before we start analyzing a lot of facts and figures, let me clarify a few important points:

- Debt refers to something owed as of **a point in time**. For example, as of September 30th, 2010, the debt is $13.56 trillion. Do not confuse debt with the term deficit, which is an excess of expenses over receipts over **a period of time**. There is a relationship between debt and deficits (discussed in Chapter 3).
- The Bureau of Public Debt, an agency within the U.S. Department of the Treasury, is responsible for keeping track of the U.S. federal government debt – which it refers to as the "Public Debt". I prefer, and will typically use, the term "total debt" or just "debt".
- The numbers in this book focus only on the debt of the U.S. federal government and do not include the debt of state governments or U.S. citizens.
- Fiscal Year (FY) refers to a 1-year period of time used by an organization for accounting and reporting purposes and which may or may not align with a calendar year (i.e. January 1st – December 31st). The U.S. Government's fiscal year[3] runs from October 1st – September 30th. For example, FY 2010 runs from Oct. 1, 2009 – Sept 30, 2010. FY 2011 runs from Oct 1, 2010 – Sept 30, 2011, and so on.

Let's take an initial look at the debt over the last 220 years. Table 1-1, sourced from The Bureau of Public Debt, shows debt amounts as of the end of each fiscal year.

Year	Debt	Year	Debt	Year	Debt	Year	Debt
2015	19,683,285,000,000(est.)	1955	274,374,222,803	1900	2,136,961,092	1845	15,925,303
2014	18,532,303,000,000(est.)	1954	271,259,599,108	1899	1,991,927,307	1844	23,461,653
2013	17,453,482,000,000(est.)	1953	266,071,061,639	1898	1,796,531,996	1843	32,742,922
2012	16,335,662,000,000(est.)	1952	259,105,178,785	1897	1,817,672,666	1842	13,594,481
2011	15,144,029,000,000(est.)	1951	255,221,976,815	1896	1,769,840,323	1841	5,250,876
2010	13,561,623,030,892	1950	257,357,352,351	1895	1,676,120,983	1840	3,573,344
2009	11,909,829,003,512	1949	252,770,359,860	1894	1,632,253,637	1839	10,434,221
2008	10,024,724,896,912	1948	252,292,246,513	1893	1,545,985,686	1838	3,308,124
2007	9,007,653,372,262	1947	258,286,383,109	1892	1,588,464,145	1837	336,958
2006	8,506,973,899,215	1946	269,422,099,173	1891	1,545,996,592	1836	37,513
2005	7,932,709,661,724	1945	258,682,187,410	1890	1,552,140,205	1835	33,733
2004	7,379,052,696,330	1944	201,003,387,221	1889	1,619,052,922	1834	4,760,082
2003	6,783,231,062,744	1943	136,696,090,330	1888	1,692,858,985	1833	7,001,699
2002	6,228,235,965,597	1942	72,422,445,116	1887	1,657,602,593	1832	24,322,235
2001	5,807,463,412,200	1941	48,961,443,536	1886	1,775,063,014	1831	39,123,192
2000	5,674,178,209,887	1940	42,967,531,038	1885	1,863,964,873	1830	48,565,407
1999	5,656,270,901,615	1939	40,439,532,411	1884	1,830,528,924	1829	58,421,414
1998	5,526,193,008,898	1938	37,164,740,315	1883	1,884,171,728	1828	67,475,044
1997	5,413,146,011,397	1937	36,424,613,732	1882	1,918,312,994	1827	73,987,357
1996	5,224,810,939,136	1936	33,778,543,494	1881	2,069,013,570	1826	81,054,060
1995	4,973,982,900,709	1935	28,700,892,625	1880	2,120,415,371	1825	83,788,433
1994	4,692,749,910,013	1934	27,053,141,414	1879	2,349,567,482	1824	90,269,778
1993	4,411,488,883,139	1933	22,538,672,560	1878	2,256,205,893	1823	90,875,877
1992	4,064,620,655,522	1932	19,487,002,444	1877	2,205,301,392	1822	93,546,677
1991	3,665,303,351,697	1931	16,801,281,492	1876	2,180,395,067	1821	89,987,428
1990	3,233,313,451,777	1930	16,185,309,831	1875	2,232,284,532	1820	91,015,566
1989	2,857,430,960,187	1929	16,931,088,484	1874	2,251,690,468	1819	95,529,648
1988	2,602,337,712,041	1928	17,604,293,201	1873	2,234,482,993	1818	103,466,634
1987	2,350,276,890,953	1927	18,511,906,932	1872	2,253,251,329	1817	123,491,965
1986	2,125,302,616,658	1926	19,643,216,315	1871	2,353,211,332	1816	127,334,934
1985	1,823,103,000,000	1925	20,516,193,888	1870	2,480,672,428	1815	99,833,660
1984	1,572,266,000,000	1924	21,250,812,989	1869	2,588,452,214	1814	81,487,846
1983	1,377,210,000,000	1923	22,349,707,365	1868	2,611,687,851	1813	55,962,828
1982	1,142,034,000,000	1922	22,963,381,708	1867	2,678,126,104	1812	45,209,738
1981	997,855,000,000	1921	23,977,450,553	1866	2,773,236,174	1811	48,005,588
1980	907,701,000,000	1920	25,952,456,406	1865	2,680,647,870	1810	53,173,218
1979	826,519,000,000	1919	27,390,970,113	1864	1,815,784,371	1809	57,023,192
1978	771,544,000,000	1918	14,592,161,414	1863	1,119,772,139	1808	65,196,318
1977	698,840,000,000	1917	5,717,770,280	1862	524,176,412	1807	69,218,399
1976	620,433,000,000	1916	3,609,244,262	1861	90,580,874	1806	75,723,271
1975	533,189,000,000	1915	3,058,136,873	1860	64,842,288	1805	82,312,151
1974	475,059,815,732	1914	2,912,499,269	1859	58,496,838	1804	86,427,121
1973	458,141,605,312	1913	2,916,204,914	1858	44,911,881	1803	77,054,686
1972	427,260,460,941	1912	2,868,373,874	1857	28,699,832	1802	80,712,632
1971	398,129,744,456	1911	2,765,600,607	1856	31,972,538	1801	83,038,051
1970	370,918,706,950	1910	2,652,665,838	1855	35,586,957	1800	82,976,294
1969	353,720,253,841	1909	2,639,546,241	1854	42,242,222	1799	78,408,670
1968	347,578,406,426	1908	2,626,806,272	1853	59,803,118	1798	79,228,529
1967	326,220,937,795	1907	2,457,188,062	1852	66,199,342	1797	82,064,479
1966	319,907,087,795	1906	2,337,161,839	1851	68,304,796	1796	83,762,172
1965	317,273,898,984	1905	2,274,615,064	1850	63,452,774	1795	80,747,587
1964	311,712,899,257	1904	2,264,003,585	1849	63,061,859	1794	78,427,405
1963	305,859,632,996	1903	2,202,464,782	1848	47,044,862	1793	80,358,634
1962	298,200,822,721	1902	2,158,610,446	1847	38,826,535	1792	77,227,925
1961	288,970,938,610	1901	2,143,326,934	1846	15,550,203	1791	75,463,477
1960	286,330,760,848						
1959	284,705,907,078						
1958	276,343,217,746						
1957	270,527,171,896						
1956	272,750,813,649						

Table 1-1 U.S. Debt, FY1791-2015, Source: U.S. Treasury Bureau of Public Debt (FY2011-2015 Estimates)

Fiscal Year 2011-2015 amounts are estimates from the FY11 budget of The Office of Management and Budget (OMB), an entity within the Executive Office of the President. Years where the debt was reduced from the prior year are denoted in gray.

Observations

The debt has risen from $75.46 million in FY1791[4] to $13.56 trillion as of the end of FY2010 (Sept. 30, 2010). Based on current estimates from the OMB, an additional $6 trillion will be added over the next 5 years. I encourage you to spend several minutes studying Table 1-1 before continuing. Think about significant events in our country's history (e.g., major wars, depressions, etc.) and notice how the debt has changed accordingly. An online copy of this table is also available through the book's website, www.UnderstandingTheUSDebt.com.

Certainly, at first glance, the historical increase in debt is staggering – and the projected increase is difficult to imagine. Note also the debt has not been reduced even one time in the last 53 years. Though the trend seems dramatic, there are two factors to consider that may make the increase in debt somewhat less problematic – inflation and the relative growth of the U.S. economy.

Adjusting for Inflation

220 years is a long period of time, and the numbers in Table 1-1 represent the debt in terms of current dollars. Without adjusting these numbers for inflation, the increase in debt may be overstated. Inflation is defined as a rise in the general level of prices of goods and services in an economy over a period of time. The Consumer Price Index (CPI-U), published by the U.S. Department of Labor Bureau of Labor Statistic (BLS), is "a measure of the average change over time in the prices … for a market basket of consumer goods and services."[5] A common method to adjust for inflation is to divide the CPI for a historical year into the index of a more recent "base" year, with the result being multiplied against the historical amount to arrive at a "real" dollar amount. For example, to express the FY1791 debt amount of $75.46 million in September 2009 dollars, the formula would be:

1791 debt amount (in Sept. 2009 dollars) = $75.46 * (Sept. 2009 CPI / 1790 CPI)
1791 debt amount (in Sept. 2009 dollars) = $75.46 * (215.969 / 8.86)
1791 debt amount (in Sept. 2009 dollars) = $75.46 * (24.3757)
1791 debt amount (in Sept. 2009 dollars) = $1.84 billion

The graph in Figure 1-1 plots the historical debt in both current and "real" (Sept. 2009) dollar amounts. Analyzing the graph brings us to the same conclusion – even after factoring for inflation, the increase in debt is dramatic. The inflation adjusted numbers show the impact of World War I, the Great Depression, and World War II but the general trend, certainly since the 1970's, is the same.

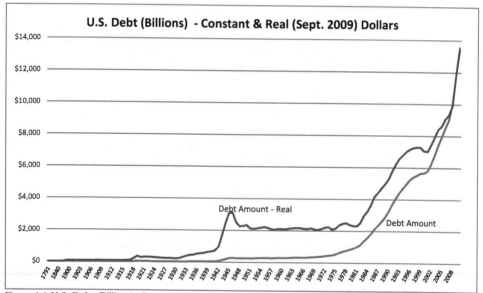

Figure 1-1 U.S. Debt (Billions), Constant and Real (Sept. 2009) Dollars, Source: U.S. Treasury Bureau of Public Debt; real amounts computed with CPI-U values from U.S. Department of Labor BLS

Debt as a Percentage of Gross Domestic Product

Consider two individuals, each with credit card debt of $35,000:
  -A single man with an annual income of $350,000
  -A married man with 5 children, a stay-at-home wife, and an annual income of $42,000.

With a debt to income ratio of 10% ($35,000 / $350,000), the single man's debt problem seems less burdensome than the married man whose ratio is 83%. Similar reasoning would suggest a country with a large economy can shoulder a large debt compared to a country with a small economy. So the rise in debt may not be as problematic if the size of our economy is also growing at a similar, or hopefully more rapid, pace. In economic analysis, debt is often expressed as a percentage of a country's Gross Domestic Product (GDP). GDP, a basic measure of a country's economic performance, is defined as "the market value of all final goods and services made within the borders of a nation in a year."[6]

There are potential flaws in this reasoning. GDP is not the same thing as a country's income (taxes) though there is a strong correlation between the two. Nor is GDP necessarily an indicator of the net funds available (i.e. income less expenses) to pay off debt. In my example of the two individuals, the single man may be living beyond his means with an expensive house payment, alimony and child support, country club memberships, etc. The married man, on the other hand, may own his home outright and live very frugally. His wife and children may even be able to work part time to generate additional income. Whose debt problem is more burdensome?

But, for now, let us use GDP (published by The Bureau of Economic Analysis[7]) to understand how our debt has changed relative to the economy. Figure 1-2 shows the debt as a percentage of GDP.

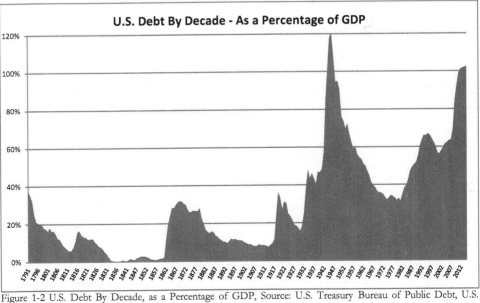

Figure 1-2 U.S. Debt By Decade, as a Percentage of GDP, Source: U.S. Treasury Bureau of Public Debt, U.S. Bureau of Economic Analysis (GDP)

Rather than many decades of a relatively low debt level, followed by a steady and then a very dramatic increase, we instead see a value that tends to rise and fall over time. If we imagine figure 1-2 as an ocean wave, the wave often rises suddenly and then gradually falls back down. For example, in FY1791 debt as a percentage of GDP was 38%. Twenty years later the ratio had dropped to less than 8%. Similarly, the Civil War quickly pushed the debt ratio to over 30%; by the 1900's, the ratio fell back to 8%. During World War II, the ratio spiked as high as 121% in FY1946.

Recent history, however, reveals a troublesome pattern. Going back to the wave analogy, the wave over time is getting larger. Since FY1933, the debt ratio has stayed above 30%. Furthermore, there isn't always a sudden rise in the debt ratio. From FY1981 to FY1993, the ratio steadily increased over twelve years – doubling from 31% to 64%. And with the exception of a 5 year decrease (FY1997-2001) the ratio has been on a steady rise, increasing from 36% in FY1970 to 92% in FY2010 – with an estimated rise to 102.6% by FY2015.

To conclude, the rising debt is rising faster than the economy. The reasons for this increase are not always obvious.

Historical Analysis

As we've already seen, historical surges in debt often coincide with major events. For example, look at the time period from 1791-1859 shown in figure 1-3. The initial debt amount of $75 million, which was a result of the Revolutionary War, stayed fairly constant for about a decade, though as a percentage of GDP it fell considerably. A recession in 1802 caused a brief rise, but then the debt was reduced to $45 million by 1812.

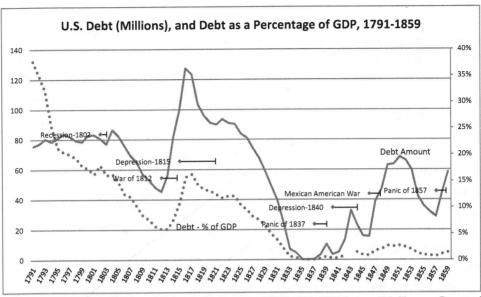

Figure 1-3 U.S. Debt (Millions), and Debt as a Percentage of GDP 1791-1859, Source: U.S. Treasury Bureau of Public Debt, U.S. Bureau of Economic Analysis (GDP). Historical Events sourced from www.historycentral.com/wars.html and http://en.wikipedia.org/wiki/List_of_recessions_in_the_United_States

The War of 1812 followed by a depression in 1815 caused the debt to spike to $127 million. Then, during a relatively quiet twenty year period, in terms of wars and financial calamities, the U.S. debt was **eliminated** in FY1835[8].

The panic of 1837, a severe depression in 1840, and the Mexican American War in 1846-1848 pushed the debt back to $68 million by 1851. In the next six years, the debt was reduced to $28 million before the next financial crisis, the panic of 1857.

For the next 110 years of history, we continue to see the same pattern, as shown in figures 1-4 and 1.5. Major wars and financial events pushed the debt or debt as a percentage of GDP upwards, but then one or both values started to gradually fall back down. As expected, financial recessions tend to have a smaller effect than wars, financial depressions, and panics.

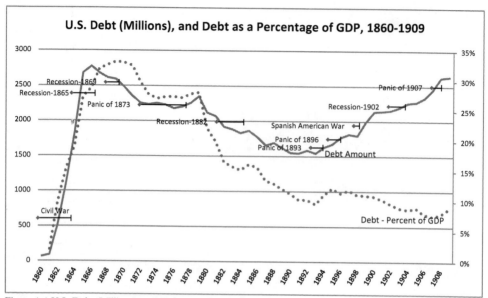

Figure 1-4 U.S. Debt (Millions), and Debt as a Percentage of GDP 1860-1909, Source: U.S. Treasury Bureau of Public Debt, U.S. Bureau of Economic Analysis (GDP)

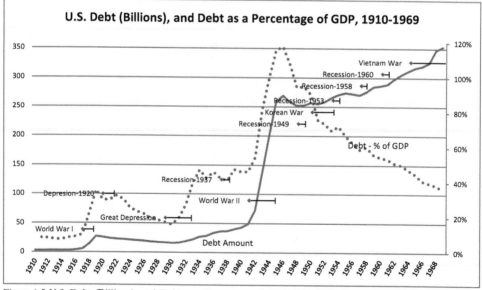

Figure 1-5 U.S. Debt (**Billions**), and Debt as a Percentage of GDP 1910-1969, Source: U.S. Treasury Bureau of Public Debt, U.S. Bureau of Economic Analysis (GDP)

Starting in 1970, the pattern changes. The debt and debt as a percentage of GDP, with the exception of a dip in the late 1990's, rise at an increasing pace, irrespective of events. Military conflicts and financial recessions exacerbate but do not dictate the pattern, and there is no gradual decline afterwards.

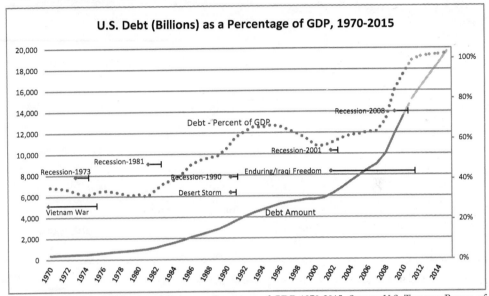

Figure 1-6 U.S. Debt (**Billions**), and Debt as a Percentage of GDP 1970-2015, Source: U.S. Treasury Bureau of Public Debt, U.S. Bureau of Economic Analysis (GDP)

Blame it on the Founding Fathers?

Last year I came across an Associated Press article entitled "Economists point to rising debt as next crisis, higher taxes and reduced federal benefits, services may be result."[9] The article was picked up by several major news media outlets, and I was intrigued by its introduction,

> *The Founding Fathers left one legacy not celebrated on Independence Day but which affects us all. It's the national debt.*

In terms of historical context, the author included a quote from Alexander Hamilton, who stated "A national debt, if not excessive, will be to us a national blessing." I want to point out two misconceptions in this article. First of all, the debt of the Founding Fathers was paid off in FY1835. We cannot blame our current problems on them.

Secondly, Alexander Hamilton was one of many Founding Fathers[10]. My research indicates several of our founders, including George Washington, Benjamin Franklin, and Thomas Jefferson, despised debt and consistently warned against it at both a personal and corporate level[11]. They also did not believe that debts should be passed on from one generation to the next. Thomas Jefferson stated,

> *That we are bound to defray [the war's] expenses within our own time, and unauthorized to burden posterity with them, I suppose to have been proved in my former letter…. We shall all concern ourselves morally bound to pay them ourselves; and consequently within the life [expectancy] of the majority.[12]*

Current views on debt are different not only from the Founding Fathers but even generations from just a hundred years ago. For example, the Sears mail-order catalog was introduced in 1886. It wasn't until 1911 they even began extending credit to customers[13]. If you have living great-grandparents, ask them about their views of debt and buying on credit. I imagine their opinions will be much different than that of younger Americans.

Summary

In May 2010 riots in Greece erupted over their debt-induced economic crisis.[14] Some people commented the United States could soon follow in Greece's footsteps. Several other European countries did have debt problems and riots of their own in 2010, including Spain, France, and Italy. As one radio host noted, when a smaller European country has a debt crisis, the rest of the world watches. But if the United States ends up in a debt crisis, the rest of the world will suffer. No matter how you analyze the U.S. debt, its size and rate of increase is problematic.

Chapter 2 – The Components of the Debt

—

"List your debts...in order." – Step 2 of 7, Dave Ramsey's financial peace

Introduction

If an individual wants to get out of debt, a good starting point is to take stock of major liabilities such as credit card balances, automobile and home loans, etc. This exercise helps identify and prioritize debts to be reduced or eliminated, and often sheds light on the behavior or events that led to the debt in the first place. We should be able to apply the same principle to the U.S. government. Figure 2-1, from the Bureau of the Public Debt, summarizes the debt as of the end of FY2010[15].

Note – While not shown in figure 2-1, The Monthly Statement of the Public Debt also contains an additional table with information about the *Statutory Debt Limit* – a ceiling introduced in 1917, designed to contain the debt. This limit has been raised several times in recent history.[16]

Date	Debt Limit Raised to
October 2008	$11.3 trillion
February 2009	$12.1 trillion
December 2009	$12.4 trillion
February 2010	$14.3 trillion

As of early 2011, Congress is debating whether to raise the limit again. For all practical purposes, this ceiling is now totally ineffective in containing the debt.

MONTHLY STATEMENT OF THE PUBLIC DEBT
OF THE UNITED STATES
SEPTEMBER 30, 2010

TABLE I -- SUMMARY OF TREASURY SECURITIES OUTSTANDING, SEPTEMBER 30, 2010

(Millions of dollars)

Title	Amount Outstanding		Totals
	Debt Held By the Public	Intragovernmental Holdings	
Marketable:			
Bills	1,783,675	4,778	1,788,453
Notes	5,252,585	3,301	5,255,886
Bonds	846,054	3,853	849,908
Treasury Inflation-Protected Securities	593,614	225	593,840
Federal Financing Bank [1]	0	10,239	10,239
Total Marketable [a]	8,475,928	22,397 [2]	8,498,325
Nonmarketable:			
Domestic Series	29,995	0	29,995
Foreign Series	4,186	0	4,186
R.E.A. Series [2t]	0	0	0
State and Local Government Series	193,208	0	193,208
United States Savings Securities	188,796	0	188,796
Government Account Series	129,355	4,515,925	4,645,280
Hope Bonds [19]	0	493	493
Other	1,340	0	1,340
Total Nonmarketable [b]	546,880	4,516,418	5,063,298
Total Public Debt Outstanding	9,022,808	4,538,815	13,561,623

Figure 2-1 Monthly Statement of the Public Debt of the United States, September 2010, Source: U.S. Treasury Bureau of Public Debt

The treasury securities, in the rows of Table 1 (figure 2-1), are divided into two types:[17]

Marketable – Treasury Bills, Notes, Bonds, and TIPS securities where the ownership can be transferred from one person or entity to another. They can also be traded on the secondary market.

Nonmarketable – Savings Bonds, Government Account Series, and State and Local Government Series securities where legal ownership cannot be transferred.

For the most part, these two security types represent a method of financing and are not of interest to our analysis. Along the table columns, the debt is further divided into two categories:

Debt Held By the Public – "all federal debt held by individuals, corporations, state or local governments, foreign governments, Government Account Series Deposit Funds, and other entities outside the United States Government less Federal

Financing Bank (FFB) securities." To clarify, this debt is the result of the Treasury Department borrowing money to finance operations by selling securities to the public.

Intragovernmental Holdings – "Government Account Series securities held by Government trust funds, revolving funds, and special funds; and Federal Financing Bank securities. A small amount of marketable securities are held by government accounts." This debt, held by government entities, primarily consists of fund balances.

Analysis –Debt Held By the Public

For now, there isn't much to learn about the debt held by the public, other than to understand who owns it. The Financial Management Service, a bureau within the U.S. Treasury, provides a breakdown of estimated public debt ownership[18] as shown in figure 2-2.

Summary of TABLE OFS-2.—Estimated Ownership of U.S. Treasury Securities

[In billions of dollars. Source: Office of Debt Management, Office of the Under Secretary for Domestic Finance]

FY	Total debt	Federal Reserve & Intragov Holdings	Debt held by public	Depository institutions	U.S. savings bonds	Pension Funds Private	Pension Funds State & local govt.	Insurance companies	Mutal funds	State & local govt.	Foreign & intl	Other investors
1985	1,823.1	484.9	1,338.2		78.2			73.4		284.5	222.9	328.2
1986	2,125.3	572.0	1,553.3		87.1			93.8		403.6	265.5	347.0
1987	2,350.2	669.5	1,680.7		98.5			106.2		489.0	279.5	342.6
1988	2,602.3	781.1	1,821.2		107.8			115.9		487.4	345.9	396.7
1989	2,857.4	899.1	1,958.3	205.4	115.7	119.5	129.4	121.2	120.4	359.8	391.8	395.1
1990	3,233.3	1,026.0	2,207.3	214.8	123.9	126.5	146.4	136.4	147.6	407.3	463.8	440.7
1991	3,665.3	1,166.9	2,498.4	251.7	135.4	126.2	140.2	171.4	199.5	430.2	506.3	537.6
1992	4,064.6	1,282.4	2,782.2	337.1	150.3	120.0	166.4	194.8	245.1	429.3	562.8	576.5
1993	4,411.5	1,422.2	2,989.3	366.2	169.1	125.1	188.7	229.4	283.9	434.0	619.1	573.9
1994	4,692.8	1,562.8	3,130.0	364.0	178.6	135.9	191.9	243.7	265.3	398.2	682.0	670.4
1995	4,974.0	1,688.0	3,286.0	330.8	183.5	141.4	193.0	245.2	272.6	304.3	820.4	794.8
1996	5,323.2	1,892.0	3,431.2	296.6	187.0	139.3	203.5	214.1	315.8	257.0	1,102.1	715.8
1997	5,413.1	2,011.5	3,401.6	292.8	186.2	141.6	219.7	187.3	311.4	237.7	1,230.5	594.3
1998	5,526.2	2,213.0	3,313.2	244.4	186.0	150.6	211.2	151.3	319.7	266.4	1,224.2	559.4
1999	5,656.3	2,480.9	3,175.4	239.9	186.3	167.4	217.3	130.6	338.3	271.6	1,281.3	342.7
2000	5,674.2	2,737.9	2,936.3	220.5	184.3	147.9	185.5	113.7	207.8	307.9	1,038.8	529.9
2001	5,807.5	3,027.8	2,779.7	189.1	186.4	149.9	166.8	106.8	234.1	321.2	992.2	433.1
2002	6,228.2	3,303.5	2,924.8	209.3	193.3	154.5	156.3	130.4	256.8	338.6	1,188.6	297.0
2003	6,783.2	3,515.3	3,268.0	146.8	201.5	167.7	155.5	137.4	287.1	357.7	1,443.3	371.1
2004	7,379.1	3,772.0	3,607.0	138.5	204.1	174.0	140.8	147.4	255.0	381.7	1,794.5	371.0
2005	7,932.7	4,067.8	3,864.9	125.3	203.6	184.2	164.8	159.0	244.7	467.6	1,929.6	386.0
2006	8,507.0	4,432.8	4,074.2	113.5	203.6	201.9	155.6	160.6	235.7	502.1	2,025.3	475.8
2007	9,007.7	4,738.0	4,269.7	119.6	197.1	246.7	165.6	133.4	306.3	541.4	2,285.3	324.1
2008	10,024.7	4,692.7	5,332.0	130.0	194.2	292.5	171.6	140.6	656.1	499.3	2,799.5	448.3
2009	11,909.8	5,127.1	6,782.7	199.0	192.4	324.5	176.7	196.3	643.0	502.5	3,497.4	1,050.9
2010	13,561.6	5,350.5	8,211.1	269.8	189.6	531.9	174.5	261.8	637.7	511.8	4,200.0	1,269.4

Figure 2-2 Estimated Ownership of the debt held by the public, FY 1985-2010, Source: U.S. Treasury Financial Management Service

Since 1985, foreign ownership has increased from 16% to over 51%[19]. The Treasury Department also keeps track of the major foreign debt holders. Figure 2-3 shows foreign owners by dollar amount and relative percentage value as of October 2010. Figure 2-4[20] shows how these percentages have changed over time.

China is the largest foreign debt holder, surpassing Japan in 2008. We can likely assume the Chinese government, rather than corporations and citizens, owns most of it. In terms of eliminating or reducing the debt, it really doesn't matter if it is owned by China or Chile. However, China's values and communist government are at odds with the United States. Therefore, as with any debtor/creditor relationship, we are putting ourselves in a position of increasing weakness.

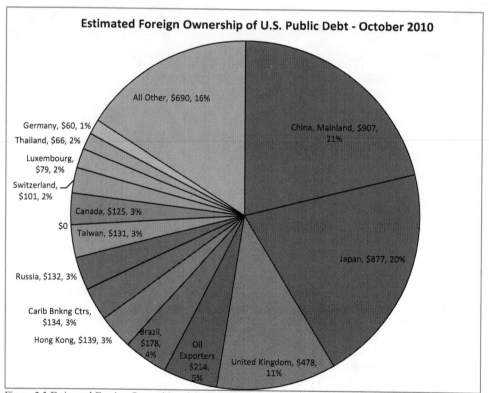

Figure 2-3 Estimated Foreign Ownership of the U.S. Public Debt (Billions of dollars and Percentage value), Oct. 2010, Source: U.S. Treasury Financial Management Service

Country	1978	1984	1989	1994	2000	2001	2002	2003	2004	2005	2006	2007	2008	2009	2010
China, Mainland	0%	0%	0%	0%	6%	8%	10%	10%	12%	15%	19%	20%	24%	24%	21%
Japan	12%	10%	21%	18%	31%	31%	31%	36%	37%	33%	30%	25%	20%	21%	20%
United Kingdom	13%	16%	13%	14%	5%	4%	7%	5%	5%	7%	4%	7%	4%	5%	11%
Oil Exporters	19%	17%	6%	4%	5%	4%	4%	3%	3%	4%	5%	6%	6%	6%	5%
Brazil	0%	0%	0%	0%	0%	0%	1%	1%	1%	1%	2%	6%	4%	5%	4%
Hong Kong	0%	0%	0%	0%	4%	5%	4%	3%	2%	2%	3%	2%	3%	4%	3%
Carib Bnkng Ctrs	0%	0%	0%	0%	0%	0%	0%	0%	0%	0%	0%	0%	0%	0%	3%
Russia	0%	0%	0%	0%	0%	0%	0%	0%	0%	0%	0%	1%	4%	4%	3%
Taiwan	0%	0%	2%	3%	3%	3%	3%	3%	4%	3%	3%	2%	2%	3%	3%
Carib Bnking Ctrs	0%	0%	0%	0%	4%	3%	4%	3%	3%	4%	3%	5%	6%	3%	0%
Canada	8%	8%	8%	5%	1%	1%	1%	2%	2%	1%	1%	1%	0%	1%	3%
Switzerland	13%	8%	4%	5%	2%	2%	3%	3%	2%	2%	2%	2%	2%	2%	2%
Luxembourg	0%	0%	0%	3%	3%	2%	2%	2%	2%	2%	3%	3%	3%	2%	2%
Thailand	0%	0%	0%	0%	1%	2%	1%	1%	1%	1%	1%	1%	1%	1%	2%
Germany	9%	11%	7%	5%	5%	5%	3%	3%	3%	2%	2%	2%	2%	1%	1%
All Other	25%	29%	39%	44%	30%	31%	27%	25%	23%	22%	22%	18%	18%	17%	16%

Figure 2-4 Estimated Foreign Ownership of the U.S. Public Debt (Percentage of Total), FY1979-2010, Source: U.S. Treasury Financial Management Service.

Analysis – Intragovernmental Holdings

Intragovernmental holdings are not a case of the government simply owing money to itself. We can't assume this debt is less important or more easily eliminated than debt held by the public. Figure 2-1 shows there are $4.515 trillion in Government Account Series securities held by "...trust funds, revolving funds, and special funds." Each of these funds effectively represents a loan, an obligation to make future payments, typically to individuals.

We've learned something important. A third of the debt is associated with funds that are part of pensions and ongoing entitlement programs. Figure 2-5 shows the top 15 of the 127 outstanding Government Account Series - Intragovernmental Holding loans as of September 2010.

Loan Description	Amount (Millions)	Percent of Total
Federal Old-Age and Survivors Insurance Trust Fund	2,399,111	53.1 (53.1)
Civil Service Retirement and Disability Fund, Office of Personnel Management	770,126	17.1 (70.2)
Department of Defense Military Retirement Fund	282,006	6.2 (76.4)
Federal Hospital Insurance Trust Fund	279,475	6.2 (82.6)
Federal Disability Insurance Trust Fund	187,222	4.1 (86.8)
Department of Defense, Medicare Eligible Retiree Fund	142,289	3.2 (89.9)
Federal Supplementary Medical Insurance Trust Fund	70,982	1.6 (91.5)
Nuclear Waste Disposal Fund, Department of Energy	47,578	1.1 (92.5)
Postal Service Retiree Health Benefits Fund	42,115	0.9 (93.5)
Employees' Life Insurance Fund, Office of Personnel Management	37,605	0.8 (94.3)
Deposit Insurance Fund	37,441	0.8 (95.1)
Highway Trust Fund	24,455	0.5 (95.7)
Exchange Stabilization Fund, Office of the Secretary, Treasury	20,436	0.5 (96.1)
Unemployment Trust Fund	18,703	0.4 (96.5)
Employees' Health Benefits Fund, Office of Personnel Management	16,242	0.4 (96.9)

Figure 2-5, Fifteen largest Government Account Series - Intragovernmental Holdings, Sept. 2010, Source: U.S. Treasury Bureau of Public Debt

The largest of these loans, the Federal Old-Age and Survivors Insurance Trust Fund, is what most of us think of as Social Security. Specifically, this fund is set up to facilitate payments to retirees and their dependents[21]. Social Security, along with Medicare, also consists of the:

- *Federal Hospital Insurance Trust Fund* – pays inpatient hospital expenses
- *Federal Disability Insurance Trust Fund* – pays benefits to disabled-worker beneficiaries and their spouses and children
- *Federal Supplementary Medical Insurance Trust Fund* - pays doctor bills and other outpatient expenses

Social Security/Medicare is 65% of intragovernmental holdings and 22% of the total debt. With such a large amount of fund obligations, it would be interesting to see how this portion of the debt has changed over time. Figure 2-6 delineates between the two debt categories from fiscal years 1953-2015 (1953 is the oldest available data from the Treasury Department). Intragovernmental holdings accounted for 15% of the total debt in 1953, rising to 44% in 2007. While this percentage value drops after 2007, it is only because the debt amount held by the public rises so dramatically.

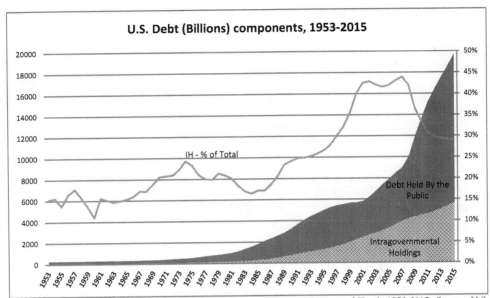

Figure 2-6 U.S. Debt (Billions), with Intragovernmental Holdings as Percent of Total, 1953-2015, Source: U.S. Treasury Bureau of Public Debt

The sheer number of loans (127) is also troublesome considering that in 1953 there were only sixteen.

Title	June 30, 1954		June 30, 1953	
	Average interest rate	Amount outstanding	Average interest rate	Amount outstanding
Special issues:				
Adjusted service certificate fund	4.000	4,643,000.00	4.000	5,113,000.00
Canal Zone, Postal Savings System	2.000	1,050,000.00	2.000	1,050,000.00
Civil service retirement fund	3.998	5,838,946,000.00	3.998	5,585,718,000.00
Farm tenant mortgage insurance fund	3.000	1,250,000.00	2.000	1,250,000.00
Federal Deposit Insurance Corporation	2.000	891,600,000.00	2.000	846,400,000.00
Federal home loan banks	1.537	231,600,000.00	2.000	50,000,000.00
Federal Housing Administration funds	2.000	14,850,000.00	2.000	25,450,000.00
Federal old-age and survivors insurance trust fund	2.250	17,054,405,000.00	2.375	15,531,700,000.00
Federal Savings and Loan Insurance Corporation	2.000	84,440,000.00	2.000	60,740,000.00
Foreign Service retirement fund	3.989	15,229,400.00	3.965	16,129,900.00
Government life insurance fund	3.500	1,234,000,000.00	3.500	1,299,000,000.00
National service life insurance fund	3.000	5,272,479,000.00	3.000	5,249,479,000.00
Postal Savings System	2.000	212,090,000.00	2.000	451,000,000.00
Railroad retirement account	3.000	3,345,255,000.00	3.000	3,127,803,000.00
Unemployment trust fund	2.250	8,024,000,000.00	2.375	8,287,000,000.00
Veterans special term insurance fund	2.000	3,025,000.00	2.125	425,000.00
Total special issues	2.671	42,228,772,400.00	2.751	40,538,257,900.00

Figure 2-7 Summary of Public Debt and Guaranteed Obligations Outstanding – FY1953, 1954, Source: U.S. Treasury Bureau of Public Debt

The rise in intragovernmental holdings explains why in recent history the correlation between the debt and military conflicts/financial recessions has grown weaker. But how can programs like Social Security and Medicare drive up the national debt? After all, Americans pay into these systems via payroll taxes and the government invests this money for future beneficiaries. There should be a corresponding set of assets in these funds to offset the amount outstanding – right?

The Ponzi scheme

In 1919, Charles Ponzi lured New Yorkers with an opportunity to earn a 50% return in 45 days by investing in foreign postage coupons.[22] Claiming he could redeem the coupons in the United States for much higher than the overseas purchase amount, Ponzi promised a doubling of investors' money every three months. Mr. Ponzi, described as a flamboyant con man, was able to attract his initial set of investors through charisma. Then, as more and more people heard about the chance to "get rich quick," millions of dollars began to flow in each week. Ponzi was able to pay off initial investors with the new money coming in, which for a time gave credibility to his claims. The investments, however, were a fraud, and he was eventually arrested. Most of the investors lost all of their money.

Ponzi schemes are also called pyramid schemes, denoting the shape and growing layers of people needed to make the scheme work. Payouts are made out of new investors' principal, not from actual profits. The schemes collapse when new investors dry up or if older investors start withdrawing money too quickly. Modern day Ponzis include Alan Stanford and Berni Madoff.

Since its inception, the "investments" made by U.S. citizens into Social Security, via payroll taxes, have never been invested; they're spent immediately by the U.S. Government on other programs. Current Social Security benefits are paid with incoming Social Security collections. Like a Ponzi scheme, Social Security has run into problems. Because of changes in birth rates, there are not enough new investors to pay for the older investors (i.e. members of the Baby Boomer generation now reaching retirement age). The older investors are also withdrawing more funds than expected, as they are living longer than past generations.

A Trust Fund?

The Social Security Trust Fund balances grow when yearly contributions exceed benefit payments. These surpluses are "invested" in Government Account Series (GAS) securities issued by the Treasury Department; the Treasury Department even pays interest on these securities by issuing additional securities.

While the Social Security Administration insists GAS securities are viable assets[23], this is merely an accounting sleight-of-hand. The GAS securities are effectively an IOU, written by the government to the government. However, because the fund balances represent obligations to individuals and not to the government, the debt is real. Recently, there have been warnings about Social Security going bankrupt"[24]. According to my 2010 Social Security statement,

> *The Social Security system is facing serious financial problems, and action is needed soon to make sure the system will be sound when today's younger workers are ready for retirement. In 2016 we will begin paying more in benefits than we collect in taxes. Without changes, by 2037 the Social Security Trust Fund will be exhausted and there will be enough money to pay only about 76 cents for each dollar of scheduled benefits.*

This statement contains both truth and fiction. It is true payments will soon exceed collections, a serious problem addressed in the past through higher payroll taxes.[25] But the "balance" of the trust funds merely tracks whether incoming payments are exceeding, matching, or lagging behind outgoing benefits. There are no funds to exhaust. Social Security is not at risk of going bankrupt – it was never solvent in the first place.

Summary

Over half of the debt held by the public is owned by foreign interests, with China being the largest of these foreign debt holders. Entitlement programs and pensions now account for over a third of the total debt. Looking at the components and ownership has yielded valuable information, but we now need to examine the government's spending habits. Historical outlays and receipts are the focus of Chapter 3.

Two additional notes:

- Last year, I was reading the Treasury Department's public debt "Frequently Asked Questions"[26] web page. One of the questions asks "How do you make a contribution to reduce the debt?" The answer provides links where one can make a contribution with credit card or check. I've often wondered if this option has an impact. I found my answer in the Footnotes section of the Monthly Statement of the Public Debt. In Fiscal Year 2009, gifts to reduce the debt totaled $3 million. Contributions will not solve the debt problem.
- Social Security and Medicare are confusing systems. I believe this is intentional. I've written a short fictional story, The Parable of the Greedy Orphanage, to make them easier to understand.

The Parable of the Greedy Orphanage

—

Once upon a time there was an orphanage, which for many years was managed by responsible and wise trustees. But one day, a greedy man took control – and he soon devised a scheme to make money for himself. The man announced,

> *To be ready for the challenges of the modern world, a college degree is required. The children in this orphanage can no longer depend on the education they receive under our care; we need to help them prepare for college. A few months ago, I instituted the "Orphan Work Program" so each child can save money for his/her future (and of course help pay for the generous care they receive).*
>
> *However, we can't expect these children to save for higher education on their own. So today, the board of trustees and I are happy to announce the "Orphan College Trust Fund." Each orphan will contribute a portion of his/her earnings to the fund, which will be invested in secure, interest bearing notes. After leaving our care, they will receive a yearly stipend to help pay for college.*

The hard working orphans began contributing into the fund. But, instead of investing the money in stocks and bonds, the greedy man spent it for himself. To cover his tracks, the greedy man created a bogus financial instrument – the Safe College Asset Marketable (SCAM) security. As the first set of orphans prepared to leave for college, he announced,

> *The Trust Fund is in sound financial condition – with $100,000 in SCAMs to help our college bound orphans.*

Now it is true the greedy man did help pay for the orphans' college. He simply used the incoming contributions from the younger orphans to do so. As payments were made, and the older orphans completed their college, the trust fund balance would drop. As younger orphans contributed to the fund, the balance would rise again.

The greedy man soon left the orphanage and someone else took his place. The orphanage grew; the number of **young** orphans increased. For a time, incoming contributions exceeded outgoing payments, and the trust fund balance of SCAMs also grew. And what did the new owner do with this temporary surplus of money? He spent it on himself.

Eventually, the large number of once young orphans went to college. And something happened that no one anticipated. Rather than finishing college in four years, the orphans took five or six years to complete their degree. The orphanage didn't put a time limit on college assistance, and the state legislators who oversaw all of the orphanages in the land were not about to let the terms of the trust fund be changed.

The orphanage responded by raising trust fund contribution rates but not outgoing benefit amounts which temporarily assuaged their cash flow problems. Alas, another problem arose. The orphanage stopped growing in size. In fact, the number of **new** young orphans actually declined. The trustees lamented,

> *The Orphan College system is facing serious financial problems, and action is needed soon to make sure the system will be sound when today's younger orphans are ready for college. In 2016 we will begin paying more in benefits than we collect in contributions. Without changes, by 2037 the Orphan College Trust Fund will be exhausted and there will be enough money to pay only about 76 cents for each dollar of scheduled benefits.*

Of course, the orphanage trustees knew there wasn't really a college trust fund to exhaust. It was all based on a SCAM. Sadly, the SCAM wasn't limited to college funds. The orphanage used the same tactic for orphan medical care, employee pensions, security personnel pensions, employee life insurance, trash disposal, mail services…

Chapter 3 – Outlays (Expenses) and Receipts

—

"We must frankly acknowledge our complicity in the creation of the unconscionable budget deficits -- acknowledge our complicity and recognize, painful though it may be, that in order to seriously address the budget deficits, we must address the question of entitlements also."
— Barbara Jordan, 1992 DNC Keynote Speech [27]

Introduction

Examining spending habits is a great way to identify the causes of debt, and the government consistently spends more than it collects. The late Congresswoman Barbara Jordan accurately identified entitlements as a significant contributor to deficits. We'll soon see there are several entitlement programs causing financial problems. But I first want to explain how expenses and receipts relate to the debt.

The relationship between debt and deficits

The U.S. federal deficit is the amount by which government outlays (expenses) exceed receipts in a fiscal year. One would think the debt is the sum total of all historical deficits. However, as we learned in Chapter 2, intragovernmental holdings (i.e. trust fund balances) also are part of the debt. Therefore, yearly deficits show up as increases in the debt held by the public, and trust fund accumulations show up as increases in intragovernmental holdings. These two categories together drive the increase in the total debt.

The Treasury Department states *"You can think of the total debt as accumulated deficits plus accumulated off-budget surpluses."*[28] Though we haven't talked about "off-budget surpluses", just replace the term with intragovernmental holdings. A loose mathematical formula for the total debt is:

$$\text{total debt} = \sum \text{deficits} + \sum \text{intragovernmental holdings}$$

Figure 3-1 shows the accuracy of this formula over the last several years. The topmost solid line represents the annual deficit; it rises above zero in FY1998-

FY2001 as there was a surplus in these years. The deficits closely match the annual changes in the debt held by the public (the dotted line).

The dashed line represents the annual deficit combined with the increase in intragovernmental holdings. The bottommost line is the change in total debt. The dashed line and the total debt line closely match one another.

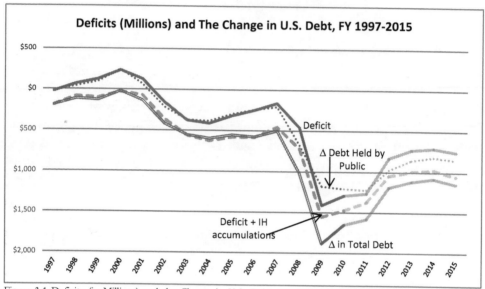

Figure 3-1 Deficits (in Millions) and the Change in U.S. Debt, FY1997-2015, Source: U.S. Treasury Bureau of Public Debt

There are reasons why these lines don't always **exactly** match. Funds from a surplus aren't necessarily applied against the debt. The government may hold the money and spend it later. Increases in the debt held by the public may not immediately show up as expenses if the government temporarily parks the money in a fund[29]. Over time, however, the formula is valid.

Historical Expenses and Receipts

At the start of the 20th century, the U.S. was in decent financial shape. The FY1900 debt of $2.1 billion was just 11% of GDP. We had eliminated $500 billion from the debt of the Civil War, despite two financial panics and a brief war with Spain (refer to figure 1-4 in Chapter 1). Expenses were 2.7% of GDP, a bit lower than the 3.2% historical average. As such, I'm not going to spend a lot of time analyzing expenses and receipts prior to 1900. While there are some great stories early in our history, including the elimination of the debt by President Jackson in the 1830's, our current problems stem from events that occurred after 1900.

Summary expense and receipt data is available from the OMB since FY1900. Figure 3-2 tracks expenses and receipts, as a percentage of GDP, from FY1900-FY2015.

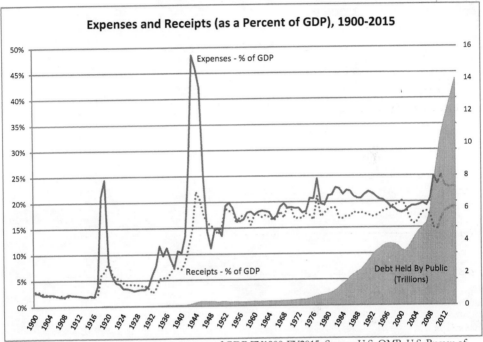

Figure 3-2 Expenses and Receipts, as a percentage of GDP FY1900-FY2015, Source: U.S. OMB, U.S. Bureau of Economic Analysis (GDP)

From 1900-1916, expenses were 2% of GDP and there were more surpluses than deficits. During World War I expenses surged, as did receipts to a lesser extent. The amount of civil and general government spending also surged during this time under President Woodrow Wilson[30]. From FY1920-1930, there were 11 straight surpluses, and receipts dropped to 3% of GDP. Expenses rose during the Great Depression, and then again dramatically during World War II. From FY1947-1960, there were an equal number of deficits and surpluses, though expenses averaged 16% of GDP. FY1960-1997 was a period of deficits (only 2 surpluses) and expenses over 20% of GDP. FY1998-2001 is actually a bright spot in recent history with four straight surpluses and a decrease in the debt held by the public. Though there were large deficits from FY2002-2005, the trend by the end of FY2007 suggested we might again be headed toward future surpluses. But, expenses rose while receipts simultaneously dropped in FY2008, and we then had the first ever trillion dollar deficits in FY2009 and FY2010. Forecasts for FY2011-2015 also call for very large deficits.

FY	Receipts	Outlays	Deficit	FY	Receipts	Outlays	Deficit	FY	Receipts	Outlays	Deficit
				1979	463,303	504,028	40,725	1939	6,295	9,141	2,846
				1978	399,561	458,746	59,185	1938	6,750	6,840	90
				1977	436,791	505,193	68,402	1937	5,387	7,580	2,193
				1976	298,062	371,792	73,730	1936	3,923	8,228	4,305
2015 e	3,633,679	4,385,531	751,852	1975	279,091	332,332	53,241	1935	3,610	6,412	2,802
2014 e	3,455,451	4,161,230	705,779	1974	263,224	269,359	6,135	1934	2,956	6,541	3,585
2013 e	3,188,115	3,915,443	727,328	1973	230,800	245,707	14,907	1933	1,997	4,598	2,601
2012 e	2,926,400	3,754,852	828,452	1972	207,309	230,681	23,372	1932	1,924	4,659	2,735
2011 e	2,567,181	3,833,861	1,266,680	1971	187,140	210,172	23,032	1931	3,116	3,577	461
2010	2,161,762	3,455,982	1,294,220	1970	192,807	195,649	2,842	1930	4,058	3,320	738
2009	2,104,995	3,517,681	1,412,686	1969	186,882	183,640	3,242	1929	3,862	3,127	735
2008	2,524,326	2,982,881	458,555	1968	152,974	178,134	25,160	1928	3,900	2,961	939
2007	2,568,239	2,728,940	160,701	1967	148,821	157,464	8,643	1927	4,013	2,857	1,156
2006	2,407,254	2,655,435	248,181	1966	130,834	134,532	3,698	1926	3,795	2,930	865
2005	2,153,859	2,472,205	318,346	1965	116,818	118,228	1,410	1925	3,641	2,924	717
2004	1,880,279	2,293,006	412,727	1964	112,615	118,528	5,913	1924	3,871	2,908	963
2003	1,782,532	2,160,117	377,585	1963	106,560	111,316	4,756	1923	3,853	3,140	713
2002	1,853,395	2,011,153	157,758	1962	99,676	106,821	7,145	1922	4,026	3,289	737
2001	1,991,426	1,863,190	128,236	1961	94,388	97,723	3,335	1921	5,571	5,062	509
2000	2,025,457	1,789,216	236,241	1960	92,491	92,191	300	1920	6,649	6,358	291
1999	1,827,645	1,702,035	125,610	1959	79,250	92,098	12,848	1919	5,130	18,493	13,363
1998	1,721,955	1,652,685	69,270	1958	79,636	82,405	2,769	1918	3,645	12,677	9,032
1997	1,579,423	1,601,307	21,884	1957	79,990	76,578	3,412	1917	1,101	1,954	853
1996	1,453,177	1,560,608	107,431	1956	74,588	70,640	3,948	1916	761	713	48
1995	1,351,932	1,515,884	163,952	1955	65,451	68,444	2,993	1915	683	746	63
1994	1,258,722	1,461,907	203,185	1954	69,701	70,855	1,154	1914	725	726	1
1993	1,154,471	1,409,522	255,051	1953	69,608	76,101	6,493	1913	714	715	1
1992	1,091,328	1,381,649	290,321	1952	66,167	67,686	1,519	1912	693	690	3
1991	1,055,093	1,324,331	269,238	1951	51,617	45,514	6,103	1911	702	691	11
1990	1,032,095	1,253,130	221,035	1950	39,443	42,562	3,119	1910	676	694	18
1989	991,191	1,143,829	152,638	1949	39,415	38,835	580	1909	604	694	90
1988	909,303	1,064,481	155,178	1948	41,560	29,764	11,796	1908	602	659	57
1987	854,353	1,004,083	149,730	1947	38,514	34,496	4,018	1907	666	579	87
1986	769,214	990,441	221,227	1946	39,296	55,232	15,936	1906	595	570	25
1985	734,089	946,396	212,307	1945	45,159	92,712	47,553	1905	544	567	23
1984	666,485	851,853	185,368	1944	43,747	91,304	47,557	1904	541	584	43
1983	600,563	808,364	207,801	1943	24,001	78,555	54,554	1903	562	517	45
1982	617,766	745,743	127,977	1942	14,635	35,137	20,502	1902	562	485	77
1981	599,273	678,241	78,968	1941	8,711	13,653	4,942	1901	588	525	63
1980	517,112	590,941	73,829	1940	6,549	9,468	2,919	1900	567	521	46
								1850–1900	14,462	15,453	991
								1789–1849	1,160	1,090	70

Figure 3-3 Expenses and Receipts (Millions), FY1900-FY2015, Source: U.S. OMB

Analysis

The government has steadily increased its spending, and expenses have consistently exceeded receipts. Let's start by examining receipts. The OMB provides detailed receipt data from FY1934 while the U.S. Census Bureau provides details for prior years[31]. Figure 3-4 shows receipt sources as a percentage of GDP for FY1800, 1850, 1900, 1910, 1920, and 1930-2015. During the 1800's and early 1900's, the United States collected money primarily through excise taxes and customs. While not shown on the graph, some money was collected through land sales. Income taxes were not permanently established until 1913, and it wasn't until WWII that they became the dominant source of receipts. Since its inception, Social Security receipts have steadily risen and have now become the 2nd largest source (note – this receipt category includes Social Security, Medicare, unemployment insurance, and other retirement receipts). Corporate income tax revenue has fallen over the past 60 years as a percentage of GDP.

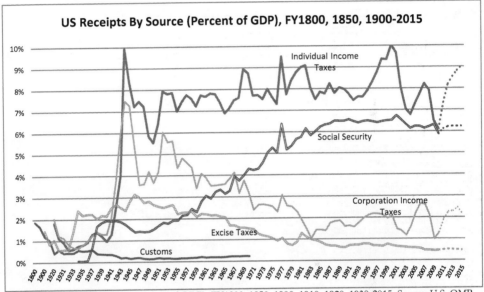

Figure 3-4 Receipts By Source (Percent of GDP), FY1800, 1850, 1900, 1910, 1920, 1930-2015, Source: U.S. OMB, U.S. Bureau of Economic Analysis (GDP)

More Taxes?

Basic math tells us our country can eliminate deficits by reducing spending or increasing revenues. Should the U.S. increase or introduce new taxes? The government could raise income tax rates on individuals and corporations, increase Social Security contributions, and create entirely new forms of taxes. Some of these ideas have been enacted or are currently under consideration[32]. But would these increases be effective at eliminating deficits? I believe they would not. I'm not going to propose we're on the wrong side of the Laffer Curve[33] and argue higher taxes will result in less revenue, though this may be true. Rather, I believe the U.S. government has a spending rather than an income problem. Referring back to figure 3-2, receipts have generally risen and fallen with expenses; expenses just tend to rise faster and fall more slowly. We need to look at expenses.

Expenses

The OMB provides detailed expense information since FY1940. Expense details are also available prior to FY1940 (through the U.S. Census Bureau[34]) although the categorizations are slightly different and less specific. Figure 3-5a shows expenses by function as a percent of GDP, while Figure 3-5b lists expenses by function as percent of total. I've included FY1800, 1850, 1900, 1910, 1920, and 1930 along with FY1940-FY2015 in both figures. Note: in figure 3-5a national defense expenses rise well above 20% of GDP during WWII (peaking at 41% in FY1943); I intentionally cut these figures off in order for the rest of the graph to be legible.

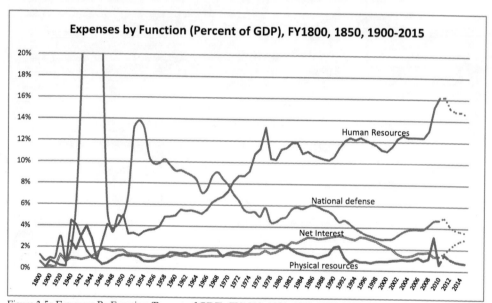

Figure 3-5a Expenses By Function (Percent of GDP), FY1800, 1850, 1900, 1910, 1920, 1930, 1940-2015, Source: U.S. OMB, U.S. Bureau of Economic Analysis (GDP). Note – Other Functions category excluded for readability.

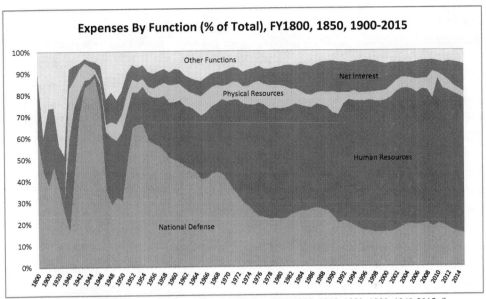

Figure 3-5b Expenses By Function (Percent of Total), FY1800, 1850, 1900, 1910, 1920, 1930, 1940-2015, Source: U.S. OMB, U.S. Bureau of Economic Analysis (GDP)

Let's define and discuss the five different spending functions.

Other Functions (5% of FY2010 expenses, 5% in FY2009)
Spending in this category includes international affairs, space and technology, agriculture, administration of justice, and general government. While it was a considerable percentage of expenses early in our history, mostly due to a lack of historical details, this category is not a large problem area today relative to other expenses.

Net interest (6% of FY2010 expenses, ~ 10% if considering trust funds)
Net interest is defined as "…interest paid by the Federal Government offset by interest collections from the public and interest received by Government trust funds."[35] The total interest expense in FY2009 was $381 billion (FY2010 details not yet available as of this writing), but $192 billion of this amount was non-cash interest expense associated with intra-governmental debt (i.e. trust funds). $192 billion was added to the trust fund balances but, as discussed in Chapter 2, this is phony interest and merely an accounting sleight of hand.

With continued deficits, interest payments will rise and eventually become the largest expense. Even without additional deficits, interest payments have the potential to increase dramatically. In 2010, the interest rate offered on a 10-year Treasury bill was a little over 3%[36]. The average rate in the 1990's was over 6%, and 10.5% during the 1980's[37]. If rates rise in the future, or if the credit rating of the U.S. government is downgraded, interest payments will skyrocket.

Physical Resources (2% of FY2010 expenses, 12% of FY2009 expenses)
Physical resource spending consists of energy, natural resources, commerce and housing credit, transportation, and community/regional development. In FY2010, physical resources were a small percentage of spending due to a credit in housing expenses. In FY2009, physical resource spending jumped to $443 billion, a 274% annual increase, due to problems in the housing market. Typically, this category is about 5% of total expenses.

National Defense (20% of FY2010 expenses, 23% if including Veterans benefits)
Historically, national defense was the primary business of the federal government. It accounted for the majority of expenses until the 1920's, and would dominate spending again during World War II and the Korean War. In recent history defense spending has hovered around 20% or less of total spending. The FY2015 forecast calls for national defense to be 15.2% of total outlays, the lowest value on record. National defense is no longer the primary business of the federal government.

Human Resources (67% of FY2010 expenses, 64% if excluding Veterans benefits)
Figures 3-5a and 3-5b reveal the fastest growing and largest area of spending is Human Resources (HR). The $2.38 trillion spent on HR in FY2010 is a 10% increase from just one year prior, and is 3.4 times greater than our national defense outlays.

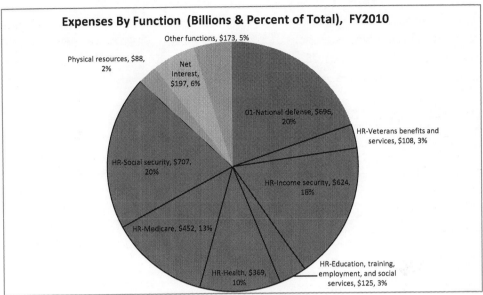

Figure 3-6 Expenses By Function (Billions and Percent of Total), FY2010

Figure 3-6 divides HR expenses into six sub-functions, defined by the government as:

- Education, training, employment and social services ($125 billion) – These programs assist citizens in developing and learning skills to expand their potential opportunities and job placement possibilities.
- Health ($369 billion) – The Federal Government helps meet the nation's health care needs by financing and providing health care services, aiding disease prevention, and supporting research and training. *(Note –approximately 75% of this category is Medicaid).*
- Medicare ($452 billion) – Through Medicare, the Federal Government contributes to the health and well-being of aged and disabled Americans.
- Income security ($624 billion) – Income security benefits are paid to the aged, the disabled, the unemployed and low-income families. Included within this classification are programs such as general retirement and disability, public assistance and unemployment compensation.
- Social security ($707 billion) – Through social security, the Federal Government contributes to the income security of aged and disabled Americans.
- Veterans Benefits and Services ($108 billion) – the VA … provides financial and other forms of assistance to Veterans, their dependents, and survivors. Major benefits include Veterans' compensation, Veterans' pension, survivors' benefits,

rehabilitation and employment assistance, education assistance, home loan guaranties, and life insurance coverage.[38]

Observations

HR spending is the leading contributor to deficits. Since 1971, when HR became and has since remained the largest spending category, we've had 34 deficits and only 4 surpluses. Few, in any, of these programs are forecasted to decrease in size. Some of them, including Social Security and Medicare, are on target to become much larger burdens in the future. And unfortunately, the government has decided to double down in HR with the recent passage of Healthcare "reform" legislation. Figure 3-7 shows the historical rise in HR spending over the last 70 years at a greater level of specificity.

	1940	1950	1960	1970	1980	1990	2000	2010	2015e
Education, training, employment, & social services	2	0	1	9	32	37	54	125	131
Elementary, secondary, and vocational education				3	7	10	21	84	46
Higher education				1	7	11	10	20	50
Research and general education aids				0	1	2	3	4	4
Training and employment				2	10	6	7	11	8
Other labor services				0	1	1	1	2	2
Social services				2	6	8	13	21	21
Health	0	0	1	6	23	58	155	369	430
Medicaid				3	14	41	118	275	336
Health research and training				2	4	9	18	33	31
Other			1	1	5	8	19	61	62
Medicare				6	32	98	197	452	659
Income security	1.5	4	7	16	87	149	254	624	538
General retirement and disability				1	5	5	5	8	10
Federal employee retirement and disability				6	27	52	77	120	141
Unemployment compensation				3	17	17	21	189	65
Food and nutrition assistance				1	13	21	28	90	90
Supplemental Security Income					6	11	30	44	52
Family and Other Support Assistance				4	7	12	21	30	25
Earned Income Tax Credit					1	4	26	50	45
Child Tax Credit							1	23	26
Making Work Pay Tax Credit								20	
Payments to States for foster care/adoption assistance						2	5	7	8
Housing Assistance and Other				0	0	0	0	32	5
Social security	0	1	12	30	119	249	409	707	900
Veterans benefits and services	0.6	9	5	9	21	29	47	108	148
Income security for veterans				6	12	15	25	63	71
Veterans education, training, and rehabilitation				1	2	0	1	9	13
Hospital and medical care for veterans				2	7	12	20	46	56
Veterans housing				0	0	1	0	1	1
Other veterans benefits and services				0	1	1	1	6	7
Grand Total - Billions	4	14	26	75	313	619	1,116	2,385	2,804
Grand Total - % of All Outlays	42%	32%	27%	37%	51%	48%	61%	67%	63%
Grand Total - % of GDP	4.5%	5.0%	5.0%	7.3%	11.3%	10.6%	11.1%	16.2%	14.6%

Figure 3-7 HR Outlays (Billions), FY1940-2015, Source: U.S. OMB, U.S. Bureau of Economic Analysis (GDP). Amounts rounded to nearest billion. Detailed outlay amounts not available for FY1940-FY1960.

The amount and rate of increase in HR spending is troublesome. Social Security and Medicare bring in additional tax revenue to help offset costs. But this revenue doesn't cover all Social Security/Medicare/Medicaid costs. To illustrate, let's recreate figure 3-2 with Social Security, Medicare, and Medicaid receipts and expenses removed through the end of FY2009.

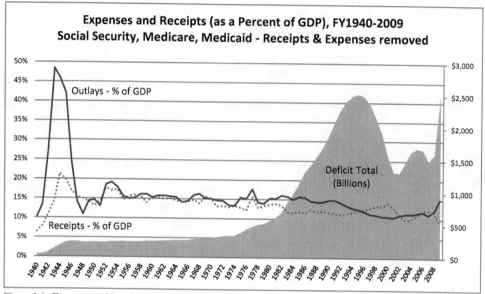

Figure 3-8a Expenses and Receipts, as a percentage of GDP FY1940-FY2009, Source: U.S. OMB, U.S. Bureau of Economic Analysis (GDP)

A few notes about the methodology used to create figure 3-8a:

- We've discussed the relationship between deficits and debt held by the public; over time, they are roughly the same. I used a running total of all estimated historical deficits to calculate a new debt held by the public.
- This is a conservative estimate in that I did not change or remove any historical interest payments. I'm using the actual interest payments, not the lower interest payments that would have occurred with lower debt held by the public balances.

In this scenario, we end up with smaller deficits and a few additional surpluses. We also eliminate $2.87 trillion in intragovernmental holdings (i.e. trust fund balances). Here is how the scenario in figure 3-8a stacks up with the actuals as of the end of FY2009:

Debt:	No Social Security, Medicare, or Medicaid	Actual
Debt Held By the Public	$2.49	$7.55
Intragovernmental Holdings	$1.47	$4.35
Total Debt (Trillions)	$3.96	$11.90

Social Security, along with Medicare and Medicaid, has contributed $7.94 trillion (67%) to our total debt as of the end of FY2009.

While we're in the realm of wishful thinking, let's redraw figure 3-2 with **all** HR expenses and receipts removed. In this scenario, I do not modify existing interest payments if there is a debt balance, but I do consider when the debt is eliminated. It happens in FY1976, so all interest payments thereafter are removed. Let me also point out I make no assumptions about investing the surpluses; instead, I assume the surplus money earns 0% interest. This is again a conservative estimate.

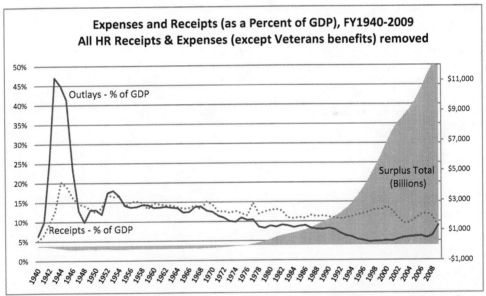

Figure 3-8b Expenses and Receipts - without HR, as a percentage of GDP FY1940-FY2015 Source: U.S. OMB, U.S. Bureau of Economic Analysis (GDP)

In this scenario, we experience only 1 deficit between FY1970 and FY2009. With all HR spending removed, we end with $11.9 trillion **in assets** rather than $11.9 trillion in debt[39]!

Government entitlement/assistance programs have proven to be a very large fiscal burden. We can't undo the past, but we'll visit this problem again in Chapter 8 to talk about future solutions. For now, let's return our attention to actual history.

The Government Snowball

In the 1700's and 1800's, large expenses were primarily the result of wars. Financing a war also left the government with large interest payments and increased Veterans benefits. But these events were temporary. The government always made a subsequent effort to pay off the debt from these events.

Starting in the early 1900's, expenses were also the result of an increasingly large government creating increasingly large programs. Figure 3-9 shows the average annual increase in what I will call general government spending, along with the start date of the large entitlement programs. This general spending includes all expenses excluding defense, interest payments, and Veterans benefits.

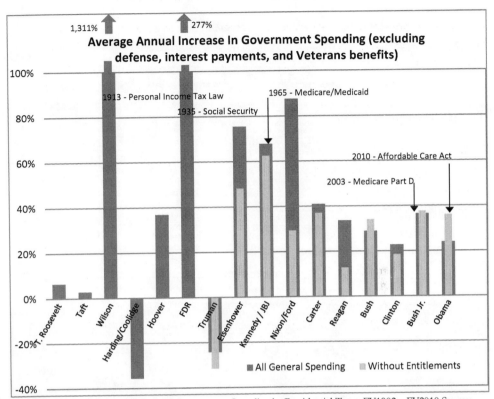

Figure 3-9 Average Increase in General Government Spending by Presidential Term, FY1902 – FY2010 Source: U.S. OMB.

President Theodore Roosevelt moderately increased government spending during his two terms in office (1901-1909). His liberal views were concerning to Republican leaders, but the real damage he inflicted was deciding to run as a 3rd party candidate in the 1913 election. By splitting the Republican vote, Roosevelt helped elect Woodrow Wilson. Wilson was an unabashed progressive, who had already changed New Jersey from a conservative state to one of the more progressive during his term as governor. In his acceptance speech for the Democratic nomination in 1912, Wilson showed his contempt for private industry,

> *Big business is not dangerous because it is big, but because its bigness is an unwholesome inflation created by privileges and exemptions which it ought not to enjoy.*

Upon winning the presidency, he made it clear America needed to be changed,

No one can mistake the purpose for which the nation now seeks to use the Democratic Party. It seeks to use it to interpret a change in its plans and point of view.

One of the first orders of change was the permanent establishment of the personal income tax, with a progressive scale for higher income earners. Though modest at first, the law was quickly changed to affect most Americans. The top marginal tax rate was increased to 77%, and collections were expanded to include steep "excess profit taxes" on corporations[40]. In 1913, $33 million was collected from income and profit taxes. By 1920, nearly $4 billion was collected.

With a new source of revenue, and using World War I as a springboard, President Wilson increased general government spending by over 1300% during his eight years in office. This is the largest increase by any President before or since, almost five times more than 2nd place finisher President FDR (no spending slouch himself).

Promoting a campaign theme of "Back to Normalcy", Americans elected Republican President Harding in 1921. Harding died after two years in office, and the frugal Calvin Coolidge served as President for the next six years. Between these two Presidents, average annual spending declined by 35%. The top marginal tax rate was reduced to 25%, and the total debt was reduced by 29%, from $23.9 to $16.9 billion. Perhaps the Roaring Twenties had something to do with a fiscally conservative government. There was even a depression from 1920-1921 that surprisingly few people have heard about. Despite the advice for government intervention by then Secretary of Commerce Herbert Hoover, President Harding knew recovery would come about through less government, and insisted that relief measures were a local responsibility[41].

Even with eight years of frugality, however, the government wasn't rolled back to anywhere near pre-Wilson spending levels. Income taxes were reduced, but they were nonexistent at the start of the century. Once a government increases in size, it is very difficult to shrink it back down. The next two presidents made no attempt to do so.

I talk about President Hoover and FDR in more detail in Chapter 6, 7, and in the Appendix. President Hoover had a chance to put his intervention theories into practice during the Great Depression. President FDR then increased general government spending by 277%. The result of this spending was a decade of double digit unemployment and a massive increase in the debt. FDR also promoted and signed into law the first major entitlement program, Social Security.

Democratic President Truman (1945-1953) reduced spending by an average of 24%, and managed to decrease the debt held by the public by 8.5%. Social Security receipts far exceeded expenses during his term, however, which meant the trust fund balances increased. The total debt amount actually rose during his presidency.

The next 57 years of history were pretty ugly. Republicans and Democrats alike engaged in significant and consistent increases in spending, and they were all saddled by growing entitlement programs. President LBJ, with his vision for a "Great Society", ratcheted up spending by over 60%. This increase excludes entitlement outlays. LBJ's vision was a form of utopia,

> For in your time we have the opportunity to move not only toward the rich society and the powerful society, but upward to the Great Society.
>
> The Great Society rests on abundance and liberty for all. It demands an end to poverty and racial injustice, to which we are totally committed in our time. But that is just the beginning.

Utopia is expensive and difficult to attain, however, so LBJ looked to pass legislation that would increase spending for years to come. Building on President FDR's New Deal, and using the Social Security Act as a foundation, he signed into law Medicare and Medicaid, now far and away the country's largest debt burden.

I review the Presidential terms of George Bush Jr. and Barack Obama in Chapter 6 and 7. I'd like to end this chapter by analyzing the spending of President Reagan and President Clinton.

The Reagan Years

When Ronald Reagan took over as President in 1981, the economy was in poor condition: 7.4% unemployment, high inflation, and interest rates approaching 20%.[42] President Reagan is credited with turning the economy around in part through marginal income tax rate deductions designed to stimulate the economy. Figure 3-10 shows expenses and receipts (in millions) from FY1977-FY1992, along with the annual percentage change in GDP. It took two years, but President Reagan's policies were successful in reviving the economy, reflected in increased receipts from FY1984 onwards. While not the focus on this book, it is worthy to note other economic indicators also improved during his tenure (e.g., by FY1989, unemployment dropped to 5.3%[43], and interest rates fell to 10%[44].

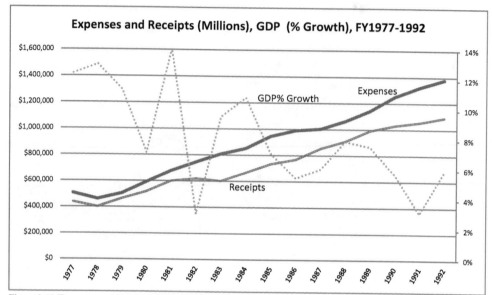

Figure 3-10 Expenses and Receipts (Millions), GDP (% Change), FY1977-1992, Source: U.S. OMB, U.S. Bureau of Economic Analysis (GDP)

Expenses also grew steadily from FY1981-1989. For example, figure 3-11 shows national defense spending nearly doubled from FY1981 to FY1989, and interest payments increased by 245%. A few other expense categories also experienced moderate to significant growth.

	1981	1982	1983	1984	1985	1986	1987	1988	1989
01-National defense	$157,513	$185,309	$209,903	$227,413	$252,748	$273,375	$281,999	$290,361	$303,559
02-Human Resources	$362,023	$388,681	$426,005	$432,042	$471,824	$481,595	$502,201	$533,405	$568,686
03-Education, training, employment, and social services	$33,152	$26,612	$26,197	$26,922	$28,596	$29,779	$28,924	$30,936	$35,333
04-Health	$26,866	$27,445	$28,641	$30,417	$33,542	$35,936	$39,967	$44,487	$48,390
05-Medicare	$39,149	$46,567	$52,588	$57,540	$65,822	$70,164	$75,120	$78,878	$84,964
06-Income security	$100,299	$108,155	$123,031	$113,352	$128,979	$120,633	$124,088	$130,377	$137,426
07-Social security	$139,584	$155,964	$170,724	$178,223	$188,623	$198,756	$207,352	$219,341	$232,542
10-Veterans benefits and services	$22,973	$23,938	$24,824	$25,588	$26,262	$26,327	$26,750	$29,386	$30,031
11-Physical resources	$70,887	$61,753	$57,604	$57,967	$56,820	$58,738	$55,143	$68,631	$81,566
19-Net Interest	$68,766	$85,031	$89,808	$111,101	$129,477	$136,017	$138,611	$151,803	$168,981
22-Other functions	$47,094	$51,068	$59,023	$55,286	$68,224	$73,724	$62,584	$57,247	$58,247
Grand Total	$706,283	$771,842	$842,343	$883,809	$979,093	$1,023,449	$1,040,538	$1,101,447	$1,181,039

Figure 3-11 Expenses (Millions) by Category, FY1981-1989, Source: U.S. OMB

In Reagan's defense, the increase in defense spending was part of his successful Cold War strategy with the Soviet Union[45]. Net interest expenses were exacerbated by high interest rates. Finally, growth in some of the expense categories (e.g., Health, Medicare, and Social Security) was automatic rather than a result of new policies. Referring back to figure 3-9, President Reagan increased general government spending, excluding entitlement spending, by a relatively modest 12%. I believe he provided a great example of how government can help repair and grow an economy. This is in stark contrast to our current situation[46]. But President Reagan did not provide the model to help us eliminate deficits and reduce the debt. He did not, or perhaps felt he could not, reduce the growth in entitlement spending.

Surpluses

What about the bright spot in recent history? Is President Clinton the model for fiscal responsibility? There were surpluses in FY1998, 1999, 2000, and 2001. Is there something we can learn from these years to apply in the future?

Figure 3-12 shows expenses and receipts (in millions) from FY1993-FY2009, along with the annual percentage change in GDP. Notice expenses rise slowly from FY1993-FY2000, and then more steadily thereafter. Changes in receipts tend to follow GDP growth. From FY1993-1997, GDP grew by an average of 5.65%. Income tax receipts grew by an average of 9.8% during this time. This economic growth, coupled with the slow increase in expenses, led to the first surplus in FY1998. GDP continued to grow 6% on average for the next three years, contributing to increased receipts and three more surpluses. Eventually, the economy cooled off in FY2001. Receipts declined as expenses continued to grow and we went back to the familiar pattern of continual deficits.

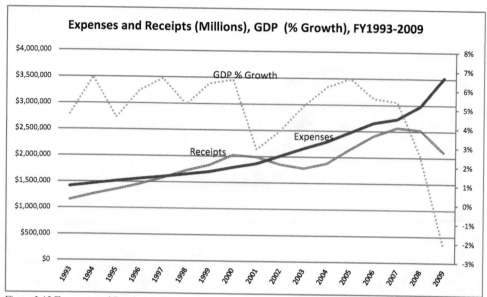

Figure 3-12 Expenses and Receipts (Millions), GDP (% Change), FY1993-2009, Source: U.S. OMB, U.S. Bureau of Economic Analysis (GDP)

So is there a lesson to be learned? Yes. If we limit the growth in expenses, there is a possibility of fiscal surpluses when the economy is doing well and there are no major military conflicts. President Clinton did a reasonably good job in limiting general government expense growth (figure 3-9). He was also able to limit spending via defense cuts as he enjoyed eight years of relative peace (defense spending was 5% of GDP and 20% of total outlays in 1993; it was 3% of GDP and 15.9% of total outlays in 2001).

But this is not a model for long-term success. Military conflicts are expensive and one of the few constants in our nation's history. More importantly, there are some expense categories that without drastic legislative changes cannot be limited. When first enacted in FY1966, Medicare expenses totaled $64 billion (.01% of GDP). In FY2010, Medicare cost $452 billion (3% of GDP). The growth in Medicare/Medicaid, along with Social Security and the new healthcare "reforms", will make it extremely difficult to limit expenses.

As with President Truman, the total debt amount continued to grow during President Clinton's term because intragovernmental holdings (specifically, the trust fund balances) increased enough to offset any surpluses. This means the government collected more in Social Security receipts than in paid out. Had this surplus money actually been invested and not spent, there would have been deficits in FY1998-FY2001.

The U.S. government simply spends beyond its means. The pattern in figure 3-12 is no different than a salesperson developing a household budget based on his best year of bonuses. He may do well for a time, but eventually the salesperson will miss quota and end up in debt.

Summary

To eliminate deficits we must create balanced budgets based on conservative receipt estimates. In the future, this will be next to impossible unless certain expense categories are drastically altered or eliminated. The current budgeting process (Chapter 5) effectively ignores several spending categories. This is unacceptable.

Entitlement and assistance programs have a way of growing quickly, costing more than anticipated, and being very difficult to get rid of. Some people advocate higher taxes to pay for these programs; I advocate living within our means. Either way, America will have to make tough decisions, perhaps changing the scope and role of the federal government along the way, if we ever hope to get out of debt.

Chapter 4 – The Actual Debt

—

"As alarming as the size of our current debt is, it excludes many items...If these items are factored in...It would take approximately $455,000 per American household [to cover these promises]."
– David M. Walker, Comptroller General of the United States

Introduction

To understand the actual financial state of the U.S. government, we need to look at more than the total debt outstanding. Consider an individual with a $10,000 credit card balance, a home loan with a $200,000 balance, and an automobile lease with $400 monthly payments. We calculate a present value of the remaining lease payments (e.g., $10,000), combine this amount with the others, and arrive at a total debt amount of 10+200+10 = $210,000.

But this isn't the complete picture. We do have assets. Perhaps the home is worth $250,000. Perhaps the credit card was used to buy electronics with some residual value ($2,000). And even though we have debt, we may also have investments (savings accounts, stocks, retirement account, etc.) worth $18,000. Ignoring asset liquidity, we have assets totaling 250+2+18 = $270,000. In this manner of thinking, we have a net worth of 270-210 = $60,000.

We need to apply the same kind of analysis to the U.S. government with the help of a balance sheet. A balance sheet, which lists assets and liabilities, is often part of a financial report. The U.S. Treasury produces an annual financial report[47], and in this chapter we'll use it to better understand the government's actual debt.

Note – I wrote this chapter using FY2009 data. In December 2010, the government released the FY2010 financial report. I've included an analysis of the FY2010 numbers at the end of the chapter.

Table 1
The Federal Government's Financial Position and Condition

Dollars in Billions		2009		2008
Gross Cost	$	(3,735.6)	$	(3,891.6)
Less: Earned Revenue	$	300.9	$	250.9
Net Cost of Operations	$	**(3,434.7)**	$	**(3,640.7)**
Less: Taxes and Other Revenue:	$	2,198.4	$	2,661.4
Net Operating Cost[1]	$	**(1,253.7)**	$	**(1,009.1)**
Assets[2]:				
Cash & Other Monetary Assets	$	393.2	$	424.5
Loans Receivable and Mortgage-Backed Securities, Net	$	538.9	$	253.8
TARP Direct Loans & Equity Investments, Net	$	239.7	$	-
Property, Plant & Equipment, Net	$	784.1	$	737.7
Other Assets	$	712.0	$	558.7
Total Assets	$	**2,667.9**	$	**1,974.7**
Liabilities[2]:				
Federal Debt Held by the Public	$	(7,582.7)	$	(5,836.2)
Federal Employee & Veterans Benefits	$	(5,283.7)	$	(5,318.9)
Other Liabilities	$	(1,257.4)	$	(1,023.1)
Total Liabilities	$	**(14,123.8)**	$	**(12,178.2)**
Net Position (Assets minus Liabilities)	$	**(11,455.9)**	$	**(10,203.5)**
Social Insurance Net Expenditures[3]:				
Social Security (OASDI)	$	(7,677)	$	(6,555)
Medicare (Parts A, B, & D)	$	(38,107)	$	(36,312)
Other	$	(94)	$	(104)
Total Social Insurance Net Expenditures	$	**(45,878)**	$	**(42,970)**
Social Insurance Net Expenditures as a % of Gross Domestic Product (GDP)[4]				
Social Security (OASDI)		-1.0%		-0.9%
Medicare (Parts A, B, & D)		-4.8%		-4.6%
Other		0.0%		0.0%
Total Net Expenditures as % of GDP		**-5.8%**		**-5.4%**

Figure 4-1 The Federal Government's Financial Position and Condition, Source: FY2009 Financial Report of the U.S. Government

The 2009 Financial Report of the U.S. Government

The government's financial report is based on its fiscal year, which as we've discussed runs from Oct. 1st – Sept. 30th. The FY 2009 report is 254 pages long; approximately 30 pages are dedicated to a Citizen's Guide[48] meant to provide an easier to understand summary. Fortunately, we don't need to look at all 254 pages. Instead, let's focus on the government's financial position and condition, shown in figure 4-1. Note this table contains a summary of assets and liabilities, taken from the government balance sheet, along with other important information.

While not critical to understanding the actual debt, let me quickly discuss the first section in the financial position and condition statement. The U.S. budget along with annual expenses and receipts are measured primarily on a cash basis. That is, expenses are recognized when paid and receipts are recognized when received. Net Operating Cost (line 5 in figure 4-1) provides an accrual rather than a cash-based means of measuring the fiscal year[49]. Accrual based accounting recognizes revenues and costs when they occur instead of when the revenues are received or costs are paid. In general, the accrual method may provide a more accurate view of an organization's performance[50]. Consider a liability incurred as the result of a program/accident/etc. If the entire amount of the liability is recognized in the current fiscal year, it is easier to 1) re-value the organization based on adjusted estimated cash flows, and 2) associate the event to a specific person/decision. In the case of the U.S. government, the 2009 financial report provides a table (figure 4-2) correlating net operating costs to annual budget deficits. In FY2009, the budget deficit of $1.4 trillion was offset by a decrease in estimated liabilities to arrive at a net operating cost of $1.2 trillion.

Table 3: Budget Deficit vs. Net Operating Cost				
Dollars in Billions		2009		2008
Net Operating Cost	$	**(1,253.7)**	$	**(1,009.1)**
Change in:				
Liabilities for Veteran's Compensation	$	(149.2)	$	339.0
Liabilities for Military and Civilian Employee Benefits	$	114.0	$	210.8
TARP Downward Reestimate	$	(110.0)	$	-
Other	$	(18.2)	$	4.5
Budget Deficit	$	**(1,417.1)**	$	**(454.8)**

Figure 4-2 Budget Deficit vs. Net Operating Cost, Source: FY2009 Financial Report of the U.S. Government

Assets

Figure 4-1 indicates the government has $393 billion in cash and cash equivalents along with an additional $2.2 trillion in other assets. Some of these other assets, however, may actually be liabilities. For example, $418 billion (or 78%) of the $538 billion in Loans Receivable and Mortgage-Backed Securities (MBSs) consists of:

- Student/education loans ($234 billion). There is uncertainty in the student loan market along with discussions of subsidies/forgiveness of loans at taxpayer expense[51].
- MBSs ($184.4 billion). As part of the 2008 Housing and Economy Recovery Act (HERA), the government effectively took control of Fannie Mae and Freddie Mac (which it refers to as housing Government-Sponsored Enterprises or GSEs). In 2009, the government purchased $181 billion of MBSs. Because of continuing problems in the housing markets, a portion of these securities may be worthless.

HERA also introduced a significant increase in government loan guarantees (a loan guarantee is a promise to assume a debt obligation in the event of nonpayment by the borrower). The Government has guaranteed $1.45 trillion in loans as of Sept 2009, as shown in figure 4-3. Note these loan guarantees do not show up on the balance sheet as assets.

Loan Guarantees as of September 30	Principal Amount of Loans under Guarantee		Principal Amount Guaranteed by the United States		Loan Guarantee Liabilities		Subsidy Expense (Income) for the Fiscal Year	
(in billions of dollars)	2009	2008	2009	2008 (Restated)	2009	2008	2009	2008
Federal Housing Administration Loans - HUD	804.2	576.4	757.3	534.9	34.1	19.6	(0.7)	(1.0)
Federal Family Education Loans - Education	457.3	414.6	445.4	405.2	20.6	43.2	(25.9)	(2.7)
Small Business Loans - SBA	74.9	75.1	62.2	61.7	4.0	1.8	4.8	0.4
Export-Import Bank Guarantees	57.7	51.8	57.7	51.8	2.2	1.4	(0.2)	-
Veterans Housing Benefit Programs - VA	183.4	220.8	50.4	63.9	3.9	3.5	-	(0.6)
Rural Housing Services - USDA	34.8	22.5	31.3	20.3	1.1	0.8	0.2	0.1
Israeli Loan Guarantee Program - AID	12.2	12.5	12.2	12.5	1.8	1.2	0.3	-
Export Credit Guaranteed Programs - USDA	7.0	3.9	6.9	3.8	0.2	0.2	-	-
Overseas Private Investment Corporation Credit Program	4.9	4.7	4.9	4.7	0.1	0.1	-	-
Business and Industry Loans - USDA	4.4	3.8	3.3	2.8	0.4	0.3	0.1	-
Federal Ship Financing Fund (Title XI) - DOT	2.4	2.4	2.4	2.4	0.3	0.3	0.1	(0.1)
All Other Guaranteed Loan Programs	18.1	14.2	16.8	13.0	0.7	0.5	0.1	-
Total Loan Guarantees	1,661.3	1,402.7	1,450.8	1,177.0	69.4	72.9	(21.2)	(3.9)

Figure 4-3 Loan Guarantees, Source: FY2009 Financial Report of the U.S. Government

Figure 4-3 indicates $69.4 billion (4.5% of the total) of these guarantees have been recognized as liabilities. The government also recognized an additional $91.9 billion in liabilities for liquidity commitments to the GSEs (i.e. providing funding advances when their liabilities exceed assets).

The government also has $239.7 billion in Troubled Asset Relief Program (TARP) related assets. TARP came about as a result of the Emergency Economic Stabilization Act of 2008 (EESA). TARP investments range from stock in troubled banks to stock in troubled automobile companies. Some of these investments may also end up as liabilities in the future.

To summarize, the government has taken over, invested, and/or committed itself to several poorly performing markets. These assets and guarantees (totaling well over a trillion dollars) may add rather than reduce the total debt in the future.

Other Assets?

The government has a very valuable asset not listed in its financial report – land. Approximately 30% of all U.S. land (roughly 650 million acres, much of this in the Western states) is owned by the Federal government.[52] The value of this asset is hard to determine, but one estimate put the land and oil/natural gas mineral rights at $975 billion in 1981[53]. This would equate to $2.26 trillion in Sept. 2009 dollars. I won't include this asset again in this chapter, but we will consider it in Chapter 8 when talking about solutions for eliminating the debt.

Liabilities

The financial position and condition statement lists total liabilities at $14.1 trillion; let's correlate this value with the total debt amount analyzed thus far throughout the book.

MONTHLY STATEMENT OF THE PUBLIC DEBT
OF THE UNITED STATES
SEPTEMBER 30, 2009

TABLE I -- SUMMARY OF TREASURY SECURITIES OUTSTANDING, SEPTEMBER 30, 2009

(Millions of dollars)

Title	Amount Outstanding		Totals
	Debt Held By the Public	Intragovernmental Holdings	
Marketable:			
Bills	1,986,173	6,334	1,992,508
Notes	3,772,964	803	3,773,767
Bonds	677,491	2,309	679,800
Treasury Inflation-Protected Securities	551,308	428	551,736
Federal Financing Bank [1]	0	11,921	11,921
Total Marketable [a]	6,987,937	21,796 [2]	7,009,733
Nonmarketable:			
Domestic Series	29,995	0	29,995
Foreign Series	4,886	0	4,886
R.E.A. Series	1	0	1
State and Local Government Series	216,488	0	216,488
United States Savings Securities	192,452	0	192,452
Government Account Series	118,636	4,335,680	4,454,316
Hope Bonds [20]	0	492	492
Other	1,466	0	1,466
Total Nonmarketable [b]	563,924	4,336,172	4,900,096
Total Public Debt Outstanding	7,551,862	4,357,967	11,909,829

Table 4-4 Monthly Statement of Public Debt of the United States Sep, 2009, Source: U.S. Treasury Bureau of Public Debt

As discussed in Chapter 2, the total debt is divided into two categories (debt held by the public, and intragovernmental holdings). Table 4-4 shows the total debt as of September 2009, $11.9 trillion. Obviously, these two totals don't match. The *Federal* debt held by the public ($7.58 trillion) in the financial position and condition statement closely matches the debt held by the public ($7.55 trillion) in table 4-4. The discrepancy appears to be with intragovernmental holdings.

As we've discussed, the bulk of intragovernmental holdings are in the form of trust fund balances. And, as I pointed out, the trust fund "balances" merely indicate whether incoming receipts are exceeding, matching, or lagging behind outgoing benefits. They're not an accurate indication of the government's true liability. Consider Social Security and Medicare. Future payments are dependent upon how long people live. The net present value of all future estimated payments less receipts is the actual liability.

The financial position and condition statement reflects the actual estimated liabilities related to federal employees and Veterans benefits ($5.283 trillion) along with $1.257 trillion in additional liabilities. These two amounts, combined with the Federal debt held by the public, add up to the $14.1 trillion in total liabilities. The financial position and condition statement calculates a net position (Assets − Liabilities) for the federal government of $2.667 - $14.123 = $-11.455 trillion.

But this isn't the complete story. The next section in the financial position and condition statement, Social Insurance Net Expenditures, calculates $45.878 trillion in "net expenditures" related to Social Security and Medicare. This number represents a liability even though the government excludes it from its net position (based on the argument the amounts are both liabilities of the Treasury and assets of the underlying trust funds). Specifically, this number is the net present value of future estimated receipts less expenses based on actuarial (i.e. life span) projections – as shown in Figure 4-5. Notice how this liability has increased by over 28% in the last four fiscal years.

United States Government
Statements of Social Insurance (Note 26)
Present Value of Long-Range (75 Years, except Black Lung) Actuarial Projections

(In billions of dollars)	2009	2008	2007	2006	UNAUDITED 2005
Federal Old-Age, Survivors and Disability Insurance (Social Security): [14]					
Revenue (Contributions and Earmarked Taxes) from:					
Participants who have attained eligibility age (62 and over)	575	542	477	533	464
Participants who have not attained eligibility age	18,559	18,249	17,515	16,568	15,290
Future participants	18,082	17,566	16,121	15,006	13,696
All current and future participants	37,217	36,357	34,113	32,107	29,450
Expenditures for Scheduled Future Benefits for:					
Participants who have attained eligibility age (62 and over)	(7,465)	(6,958)	(6,329)	(5,866)	(5,395)
Participants who have not attained eligibility age	(30,207)	(29,021)	(27,928)	(26,211)	(23,942)
Future participants	(7,223)	(6,933)	(6,619)	(6,480)	(5,816)
All current and future participants	(44,894)	(42,911)	(40,876)	(38,557)	(35,154)
Present value of future expenditures in excess of future revenue	(7,677) [1]	(6,555) [2]	(6,763) [3]	(6,449) [4]	(5,704) [5]
Federal Hospital Insurance (Medicare Part A): [14]					
Revenue (Contributions and Earmarked Taxes) from:					
Participants who have attained eligibility age (65 and over)	209	202	178	192	162
Participants who have not attained eligibility age	6,348	6,320	5,975	5,685	5,064
Future participants	5,451	5,361	4,870	4,767	4,209
All current and future participants	12,008	11,883	11,023	10,644	9,435
Expenditures for Scheduled Future Benefits for:					
Participants who have attained eligibility age (65 and over)	(2,958)	(2,747)	(2,558)	(2,397)	(2,179)
Participants who have not attained eligibility age	(18,147)	(17,365)	(15,639)	(15,633)	(12,668)
Future participants	(4,673)	(4,506)	(5,118)	(3,904)	(3,417)
All current and future participants	(25,778)	(24,619)	(23,315)	(21,934)	(18,264)
Present value of future expenditures in excess of future revenue	(13,770) [1]	(12,736) [2]	(12,292) [3]	(11,290) [4]	(8,829) [5]
Federal Supplementary Medical Insurance (Medicare Part B): [14]					
Revenue (Premiums) from:					
Participants who have attained eligibility age (65 and over)	498	461	433	409	363
Participants who have not attained eligibility age	4,224	3,859	3,184	3,167	2,900
Future participants	1,270	1,158	1,172	906	924
All current and future participants	5,992	5,478	4,789	4,481	4,187
Expenditures for Scheduled Future Benefits for:					
Participants who have attained eligibility age (65 and over)	(2,142)	(1,986)	(1,834)	(1,773)	(1,622)
Participants who have not attained eligibility age	(16,342)	(14,949)	(12,130)	(12,433)	(11,541)
Future participants	(4,672)	(4,262)	(4,257)	(3,407)	(3,408)
All current and future participants	(23,156)	(21,197)	(18,221)	(17,613)	(16,571)
Present value of future expenditures in excess of future revenue [6]	(17,165) [1]	(15,719) [2]	(13,432) [3]	(13,131) [4]	(12,384) [5]
Federal Supplementary Medical Insurance (Medicare Part D): [14]					
Revenue (Premiums and State Transfers) from:					
Participants who have attained eligibility age (65 and over)	140	123	167	173	185
Participants who have not attained eligibility age	1,442	1,380	1,627	1,700	1,790
Future participants	618	604	611	492	572
All current and future participants	2,199	2,107	2,405	2,366	2,547
Expenditures for Scheduled Future Benefits for:					
Participants who have attained eligibility age (65 and over)	(595)	(581)	(794)	(792)	(880)
Participants who have not attained eligibility age	(6,144)	(6,527)	(7,273)	(7,338)	(7,913)
Future participants	(2,632)	(2,856)	(2,699)	(2,121)	(2,440)
All current and future participants	(9,371)	(9,964)	(10,766)	(10,250)	(11,233)
Present value of future expenditures in excess of future revenue [6]	(7,172) [1]	(7,857) [2]	(8,361) [3]	(7,884) [4]	(8,686) [5]
Total present value of future expenditures in excess of future revenue	(45,878)	(42,970)	(40,948)	(38,851)	(35,689)

Figure 4-5 Excerpt from Statements of Social Insurance Present Value of Long-Range Actuarial Projections; Railroad Retirement ($100 billion) and Black Lung ($6 billion) excluded. Source: FY2009 Financial Report of the U.S. Government

Summary

Based on all of the numbers we've discussed, what is the actual debt of the U.S. government at the end of FY2009? Let's take a conservative approach and assume that all of the government's assets are indeed assets. But let us also include the estimated Social Security and Medicare net expenditures as a liability. The revised debt becomes $2,667.9 − ($14,123.8 + $45,878) = $-57.334 trillion.

This amount is nearly 5 times greater than the $11.9 trillion total debt number provided by the Treasury department. But it is an accurate assessment of our true debt. In early 2008, the comptroller general of the United States[54] David Walker came to same conclusion based on the numbers at that time. He stated to the Senate Budget Committee,

> *As alarming as the size of our current debt is, it excludes many items, including the gap between future promised and funded Social Security and Medicare benefits, veterans' health care, and a range of other commitments and contingencies that the federal government has pledged to support. If these items are factored in, the total burden in present value dollars is estimated to be about $53 trillion.*

David Walker calculated it would take "…approximately $455,000 per American household—or $175,000 for every man, woman, and child in the United States"[55] to pay off the debt.

The actual debt is much worse than we thought. As we will learn in Chapter 5, the largest debt problems are effectively ignored during the budgeting process.

FY2010 Update

Figure 4-6 shows the financial position and condition statement for FY2010. Some of the notable changes from FY2009 include:

- An increase of $1.48 trillion in the Federal debt held by the public. Most of this increase is directly attributable to the $1.29 trillion FY2010 deficit.

- A $436 billion increase in the Federal Employee & Veterans Benefits liability. $373 billion of the amount is due to an adjustment in how the VA estimates future liabilities.

- A $15 trillion **decrease** in the estimated liabilities of Medicare. This enormous adjustment, according the financial report, is attributable to the effects of the Affordable Care Act (ACA) on the Medicare program. ACA is the Health Care Reform act passed in 2010.

Table 1
The Federal Government's Financial Position and Condition

Dollars in Billions		2010		2009
Gross Cost	$	(4,472.3)	$	(3,735.6)
Less: Earned Revenue	$	309.2	$	300.9
(Loss)/Gain from Changes in Assumptions	$	(132.9)		n/a
Net Cost of Operations	$	**(4,296.0)**	$	**(3,434.7)**
Less: Taxes and Other Revenue:	$	2,216.5	$	2,198.4
Unmatched Transactions & Balances	$	(0.8)	$	(17.4)
Net Operating Cost[2]	$	**(2,080.3)**	$	**(1,253.7)**
Assets[3]:				
Cash & Other Monetary Assets	$	428.6	$	393.2
Loans Receivable and Investments, Net[4]	$	942.5	$	843.3
Property, Plant & Equipment, Net	$	828.9	$	784.1
Other	$	683.8	$	647.3
Total Assets	$	**2,883.8**	$	**2,667.9**
Liabilities[3]:				
Federal Debt Held by the Public	$	(9,060.0)	$	(7,582.7)
Federal Employee & Veterans Benefits	$	(5,720.3)	$	(5,283.7)
Other	$	(1,576.3)	$	(1,257.4)
Total Liabilities	$	**(16,356.6)**	$	**(14,123.8)**
Net Position (Assets minus Liabilities)	$	**(13,472.8)**	$	**(11,455.9)**
Social Insurance Net Expenditures[5]:				
Social Security (OASDI)	$	(7,947)	$	(7,677)
Medicare (Parts A, B, & D)	$	(22,813)	$	(38,107)
Other	$	(97)	$	(94)
Total Social Insurance Net Expenditures	$	**(30,857)**	$	**(45,878)**
Social Insurance Net Expenditures as a % of Gross Domestic Product (GDP)[6]				
Social Security (OASDI)		-0.9%		-1.0%
Medicare (Parts A, B, & D)		-2.7%		-4.8%
Other		0.0%		0.0%
Total Net Expenditures as % of GDP		**-3.7%**		**-5.8%**

Figure 4-6 The Federal Government's Financial Position and Condition, Source: FY2010 Financial Report of the U.S. Government

The ACA is projected to significantly lower Medicare spending and raise receipts though the report notes "there is uncertainty about whether the projected cost reductions in health care cost growth will be fully achieved". The Medicare and Social Security Trustees' Report[56] states,

Much of the projected improvement in Medicare finances is due to a provision of the ACA that reduces payment updates for most Medicare goods and services other than physicians' services and drugs by measured total economy multifactor productivity growth, which is projected to increase at a 1.1 percent annual rate on average. This provision is premised on the assumption that productivity growth in the health care sector can match that in the economy overall, rather than lag behind as has been the case in the past.

In other words, the ACA will somehow help facilitate "new delivery and payment models to improve the quality and cost-effectiveness of health care for Medicare — and, by extension, for the nation as a whole."[57] I believe this estimated cost reduction is completely unrealistic, and I am not alone. The U.S. Government Accountability Office (GAO) is responsible for issuing an opinion of the financial report. The GAO has effectively dismissed these new estimates,

Because of significant uncertainties, as discussed in our report, we are unable to, and we do not, express an opinion on the 2010 Statement of Social Insurance. About $22.8 trillion, or 74 percent, of the federal government's reported total present value of future expenditures in excess of future revenue for 2010 relate to the Department of Health and Human Services' 2010 Statement of Social Insurance, which received a disclaimer of opinion. In our opinion, the Statements of Social Insurance for 2009, 2008, and 2007 present fairly, in all material respects, the financial condition of the federal government's social insurance programs, in conformity with U.S. generally accepted accounting principles.[58]

Net Operating Cost

The Net Operating Cost for FY2010 of $2.0 trillion is significantly more than the $1.29 trillion deficit. When reviewing the FY2009 report, I mentioned some of the government's assets could turn into liabilities. Figure 4-7 shows two specific examples where this happened in FY2010 – $86 billion for the TARP program and an additional $268 billion for GSE's.

Table 3: Budget Deficit vs. Net Operating Cost			
Dollars in Billions	2010	2009	$ Change
Net Operating Cost	$ (2,080.3)	$ (1,253.7)	$ (826.6)
Change in:			
Liabilities for Veteran's Compensation	$ 223.8	$ (149.2)	$ 373.0
Liabilities for Military and Civilian Employee Benefits	$ 279.3	$ 114.0	$ 165.3
Liabilities for Government Sponsored Enterprises	$ 268.0	$ 78.1	$ 189.9
Downward Reestimate for TARP	$ 86.4	$ (110.0)	$ 196.4
Other, Net	$ (71.3)	$ (96.3)	$ 25.0
Budget Deficit	$ (1,294.1)	$ (1,417.1)	$ 123.0

Figure 4-7 Budget Deficit vs. Net Operating Cost, Source: FY2010 Financial Report of the U.S. Government

Chapter 5 – The Budgeting Process

–

"To contract new debts is not the way to pay old ones." – George Washington

Introduction

The need for a budget, along with reporting of receipts and expenditures, is identified in Article I, section 9, clause 7 of The Constitution of the United States:

> *[n]o money shall be drawn from the Treasury, but in Consequence of Appropriations made by Law; and a regular Statement and account of Receipts and Expenditures of all public Money shall be published from time to time.*

In a company or family, a budget is created to estimate expenses and receipts over a period of time. Typically, the goal is to stay "in the black" i.e. to make sure expenses do not exceed receipts. In the case of our government, the Executive and Legislative branches both participate in a process that has put America "in the black" only four times in the last forty years.

The budgeting process is not the most interesting thing in the world. But, the budget sets the level of annual spending, at least for certain programs. It is necessary to understand at a high level the participants and processes that consistently land us "in the red" year after year.

What is the Federal Budget?

The Citizen's Guide to the Federal Budget[59] describes the budget as:

- *a plan for how the Government spends your money*
- *a plan for how the Government pays for its activities*
- *a plan for Government borrowing or repayment of borrowing*
- *a historical record*

In describing the process, it says (with a bit of refreshing honesty),

In some ways, the Federal Government plans its budget much like families do. The President and Congress determine how much money they expect the Government to receive in each of the next several years, where it will come from, and how much to spend to reach their goals—goals for national defense, foreign affairs, social insurance for the elderly, health insurance for the elderly and poor, law enforcement, education, transportation, science and technology, and others. Unlike the Government though, a family can't just decide to take money from its neighbors when it wants to spend more than it takes in.

The federal budgeting process was formally established in 1921 with the passage of the Budget and Accounting Act of 1921[60]. The act requires the President to submit a budget to Congress each year, and it established what would eventually be called the Office of Management and Budget (OMB); the OMB's primary purpose is to assist the President in overseeing the preparation of the budget. The Act also established the General Accounting Office (GAO) as an auditor, responsible to Congress, with a mission "…to provide Congress with an independent audit of executive accounts and to report on violations of the fiscal statutes."[61]

Problems with how Congress responded to the President's budget, along with confrontations between the two branches, led to additional reform. In 1974, Congress enacted the Congressional Budget and Impoundment Control Act to take more control over the budgeting process and curb the President's impoundment (refusal to spend) powers. [62] This act established the Congressional Budget Office (CBO) to provide Congress with "Objective, nonpartisan, and timely analyses to aid in economic and budgetary decisions on the wide array of programs covered by the federal budget"[63]. It also established The House and Senate Budget Committees to coordinate the congressional consideration of the budget.

Who ultimately determines the budget? The Concord Coalition summarizes the relationship between the President and Congress,

The President's budget is presented to Congress, but the specific recommendations included in it are not binding on Congress. Since Article I of the Constitution gives Congress the power to appropriate (often referred to as the "power of the purse") Congress ultimately has the authority to determine the specific spending levels for each account. Depending on the President's standing with Congress, his budget can either be very influential or promptly declared "dead on arrival" as Presidents have often experienced when Congress is not controlled by the same political party.[64]

The President has the power to veto certain parts of the budget (which could in turn be overwritten by a two thirds majority vote) but it is Congress that controls much of the overall process.

How the Budget gets created

Ideally, the budgeting process happens over a 8 month period, as seen in table 5-1.

Due Date	Step
1st Monday in February	1. President submits Budget Proposal
April 15th	2. Congress completes Budget Resolution
June 30th	3. Appropriation Bills passed by Congress
July 15th	4. President submits Mid-Session Review
Oct 1st	5. Fiscal Year begins

Table 5-1 Summary of Budget Timetable, Source: http://budget.senate.gov/democratic/timetable.html

Step 1 – The President's Budget Proposal

Each year, the President submits a budget proposal to Congress for the upcoming fiscal year (as discussed in Chapter 1, the current fiscal year begins Oct 1st). Current law[65] requires the budget to be submitted on or after the first Monday in January but no later than the first Monday in February. The proposal tells Congress what the President recommends in terms of overall spending, estimated receipts, and the resulting deficit/surplus. By law, it includes actual expenditures/receipts from the prior fiscal year and estimated expenditures/receipts for the current, upcoming, and at least 4 fiscal years thereafter.

The current FY2011 budget proposal is publicly available as a pdf document from the OMB's website[66]. The Summary Tables are a good starting point. You can also look at the Historical Tables – an accompanying set of Excel workbooks which provide historical actuals and at least 4 fiscal years of estimates. For example, figure 5-2 is a copy of the summary budget totals table.

Table S–1. Budget Totals
(In billions of dollars)

	2009	2010	2011	2012	2013	2014	2015	2016	2017	2018	2019	2020
Budget (Without Fiscal Commission)												
Budget Totals in Billions of Dollars:												
Receipts	2,105	2,165	2,567	2,926	3,188	3,455	3,634	3,887	4,094	4,299	4,507	4,710
Outlays	3,518	3,721	3,834	3,755	3,915	4,161	4,386	4,665	4,872	5,084	5,415	5,713
Deficit	1,413	1,556	1,267	828	727	706	752	778	778	785	908	1,003
Debt held by the public	7,545	9,298	10,498	11,472	12,326	13,139	13,988	14,833	15,686	16,535	17,502	18,573
Debt net of financial assets	6,647	8,164	9,418	10,246	10,972	11,677	12,428	13,205	13,983	14,767	15,675	16,677
Gross domestic product (GDP)	14,237	14,624	15,299	16,203	17,182	18,193	19,190	20,163	21,136	22,087	23,065	24,067
Budget Totals as a Percent of GDP:												
Receipts	14.8%	14.8%	16.8%	18.1%	18.6%	19.0%	18.9%	19.3%	19.4%	19.5%	19.5%	19.6%
Outlays	24.7%	25.4%	25.1%	23.2%	22.8%	22.9%	22.9%	23.1%	23.1%	23.0%	23.5%	23.7%
Deficit	9.9%	10.6%	8.3%	5.1%	4.2%	3.9%	3.9%	3.9%	3.7%	3.6%	3.9%	4.2%
Debt held by the public	53.0%	63.6%	68.6%	70.8%	71.7%	72.2%	72.9%	73.6%	74.2%	74.9%	75.9%	77.2%
Debt net of financial assets	46.7%	55.8%	61.6%	63.2%	63.9%	64.2%	64.8%	65.5%	66.2%	66.9%	68.0%	69.3%

Figure 5-2 Partial copy of Budget Totals, FY2011 Presidential Budget Summary Tables, Source: U.S. OMB

The budget proposal further defines the President's priorities across different spending categories and government agencies. For example, Figure 5-3 breaks outlays into three major buckets – discretionary, mandatory, and interest expenses. Discretionary outlays must have their funding renewed, typically on an annual basis, via an appropriations bill (discussed in step 2) and include spending categories such as defense, health research, and transportation. Mandatory programs, while initially enacted by law, do not require an appropriation to be funded; unless specifically changed by law, spending across these categories is automatic. Social Security, Medicare, and Medicaid account for 70% of mandatory spending. Most of the remaining mandatory expenses consist of income security along with certain education and health programs (Table 5-4).

Let's pause here for a moment. Looking at the FY2011 Proposed Budget, 63% of the $3.8 trillion in total outlays is marked for mandatory spending and interest payments. An additional 23% is assigned to discretionary security (defense) spending. This effectively leaves only 14% of the budget (the non-security discretionary outlays) open for adjustment. Realize that even if **all** of this non-security discretionary spending was eliminated, we wouldn't generate even one surplus over the next ten years. Without explicit changes to the mandatory programs, there is no chance of generating a surplus.

Table S–4. Proposed Budget by Category
(In billions of dollars)

	2009	2010	2011	2012	2013	2014	2015	2016	2017	2018	2019	2020
Outlays:												
Appropriated ("discretionary") programs:												
Security	782	855	895	827	811	825	845	862	885	907	931	955
Non-security	437	553	520	475	456	457	465	475	486	497	511	529
Subtotal, appropriated programs	1,219	1,408	1,415	1,301	1,267	1,283	1,310	1,337	1,371	1,405	1,442	1,484
Mandatory programs:												
Social Security	678	715	730	762	801	845	893	945	1,002	1,064	1,130	1,201
Medicare	425	451	491	501	556	623	652	724	757	791	881	953
Medicaid	251	275	297	274	292	313	336	362	389	419	451	487
Troubled Asset Relief Program (TARP)[1]	151	−73	11	10	7	6	3	1	*	*	....	....
Allowance for jobs initiatives	....	12	25	8	3	2	....	....	....	....	....	....
Allowance for health reform[2]	....	6	−7	−17	2	30	72	101	100	100	104	106
Other mandatory programs	607	737	619	570	547	546	544	563	567	568	616	637
Subtotal, mandatory programs	2,112	2,123	2,165	2,107	2,208	2,364	2,500	2,696	2,815	2,942	3,182	3,384
Net interest	187	188	251	343	436	510	571	627	681	733	786	840
Disaster costs[3]	....	1	3	4	4	4	5	5	5	5	5	5
Total outlays	3,518	3,721	3,834	3,755	3,915	4,161	4,386	4,665	4,872	5,084	5,415	5,713
Receipts:												
Individual income taxes	915	936	1,121	1,326	1,468	1,604	1,733	1,856	1,980	2,102	2,223	2,338
Corporation income taxes	138	157	297	366	393	445	411	449	463	473	486	502
Social insurance and retirement receipts:												
Social Security payroll taxes	654	635	674	720	766	809	856	911	954	1,000	1,044	1,084
Medicare payroll taxes	191	180	192	208	223	237	251	267	280	293	307	318
Unemployment insurance	38	51	60	67	73	77	79	79	78	77	76	77
Other retirement	8	9	8	9	9	9	9	9	9	9	9	10
Excise taxes	62	73	74	81	85	87	88	89	90	90	91	92
Estate and gift taxes	23	17	25	23	24	26	28	30	32	35	37	40
Customs duties	22	24	27	32	35	37	39	42	44	47	49	52
Deposits of earnings, Federal Reserve System	34	77	79	67	59	52	48	50	52	55	57	59
Allowance for jobs initiatives	....	−12	−25	−8	−3	−2	....	....	....	....	....	....
Allowance for health reform[2]	....	....	16	18	39	58	74	86	93	101	110	119
Other miscellaneous receipts	18	18	17	17	17	18	18	18	18	19	19	19
Total receipts	2,105	2,165	2,567	2,926	3,188	3,455	3,634	3,887	4,094	4,299	4,507	4,710
Deficit	1,413	1,556	1,267	828	727	706	752	778	778	785	908	1,003

Figure 5-3 Partial copy of Proposed Budget by Category, FY2011 Presidential Budget Summary Tables, Source: U.S. OMB

Category and Program	2011 estimate (millions)
Human resource programs:	
Education, training, employment, and social services	32,512
Health:	
Other	33,409
Income security:	
General retirement and disability	6,559
Federal employee retirement and disability	123,340
Unemployment compensation	102,911
Food and nutrition assistance	95,400
Supplemental Security Income	49,450
Family and Other Support Assistance	28,742
Earned Income Tax Credit	47,233
Child Tax Credit	23,250
Recovery Rebate Tax Credit	....
Making Work Pay Tax Credit	21,429
Payments to States for foster care/adoption assistance	7,442
Offsetting receipts	-858
Housing Assistance and Other	16,263
Total income security	*521,161*
Veterans benefits and services:	
Income security for veterans	58,365
Other	10,234

Table 5-4 Other mandatory expenses, Source: U.S. OMB, Historical Table 8.5—Outlays for Mandatory and Related Programs: 1962–2015

Note – you may occasionally hear the term "on-budget" and "off-budget", and you will see these terms in several of the budget summary tables. Off-budget refers to a view of the budget that excludes Social Security[67] outlays/revenues. The idea behind this distinction is to look at the budget without factoring in the surpluses generated from Social Security. In this chapter, we are focusing on the unified budget, i.e. the entire budget.

Step 2 – Congressional Budget Resolution

After receiving the President's proposal, the Senate and the House Budget Committees each work on a draft of a budget resolution. The committees seek testimony from Administration officials, Members of Congress and expert witnesses[68]. A joint House and Senate conference is then used to produce a final resolution after working out any differences, making amendments, etc.

The budget resolution is a type of concurrent resolution in that it is passed by both the Senate and House but not presented to the President for signature. Therefore, a Budget Resolution is not a formal law but it reflects the sentiment of Congress; it serves as a blueprint for the appropriations process.

The Congressional Budget Act of 1974 requires that a budget resolution include "totals of new budget authority and outlays, total federal revenues, the surplus or deficit in the budget, new budget authority and outlays for each of the major functional categories, the public debt, and outlays/revenues for the Social Security program."[69]   There have been occasions when Congress didn't pass a Budget Resolution by the April 15th due date, in which case alternative (and less detailed) resolutions were used.[70]   This is what happened for FY2011; Congress posted something called a "Budget Enforcement Resolution"[71], but it contained only summary spending information for the 2011 fiscal year.

Like the President's proposal, the budget resolution is supposed to cover the upcoming and at least the following four fiscal years[72].   It delineates between discretionary and mandatory spending, and provides a breakout of spending across 20 functions (i.e. categories).   Notice in Table 5-5 the 20 functions roll up into 6 super functions that correlate to the categories of outlays (expenses) analyzed in Chapter 3.

Super Function	Function Code	Function
National Defense	050	National Defense
Human resources	500	Education, training, employment, and social services
	550	Health
	570	Medicare
	600	Income security
	650	Social security
	700	Veterans benefits and services
Physical resources	270	Energy
	300	Natural resources and environment
	370	Commerce and housing credit
	400	Transportation
	450	Community and regional development
Net interest	900	Net Interest
Other functions	150	International affairs
	250	General science, space and technology
	350	Agriculture
	750	Administration of justice
	800	General government
	920	Allowances
Undistributed offsetting receipts	950	Undistributed Offsetting Receipts

Table5-5 Superfunctions and Functions of budget spending.

Another important component of the resolution is the allocation provided to the House and Senate Appropriations Committees.   It is referred to as the 302(a) allocation and it sets the total amount of discretionary spending available for the year's appropriations bills.

Step 3 – Appropriation Bills Passed

Using the 302(a) as an input, Congress divides the proposed spending among twelve subcommittees[73] (referred to as 302(b) allocations). These subcommittees draft the annual appropriations bills, the laws that permit federal agencies to incur obligations and make payments.

There are currently 12 annual appropriation bills corresponding to:

1. Agriculture
2. Commerce, Justice, Science
3. Defense
4. Energy and Water
5. Financial Services and General Government
6. Homeland Security
7. Department of the Interior, environment
8. Departments of Labor, Health and Human Services, Education
9. Legislative Branch
10. Military Construction and Veterans Affairs
11. State, Foreign Operations
12. Transportation, Housing and Urban Development

The committees then send their bills to the full House and Senate, where they must be approved by a majority vote. If the appropriations bills are not ultimately passed, something called a Continuing Resolution[74] can be used to provide temporary funding based on the prior year's spending.

The appropriations bills are then sent to the President who can sign them into law, veto them, or do nothing (in which case they become law after 10 days). Congress can override a veto with a two thirds majority vote.

Step 4 – President Submits Mid-Session Review

By July 15th, the OMB, on behalf of the President, sends Congress a supplemental update of the budget. The update contains revised estimates of receipts, outlays, budget authority, and the budget deficit for the current and at least 4 future fiscal years[75]. This review contains an updated set of budget summary tables produced in step 1.

Step 5 – Fiscal Year Begins

The government's fiscal year begins on October 1ˢᵗ and the new budget is implemented.

A Note Concerning Reconciliation

Until the Health Care debate of 2010, many Americans probably never heard the term reconciliation as it relates to legislation. Defined in the Congressional Budget Act of 1974, reconciliation is designed to streamline the process of considering or passing budget and tax-related legislation. In the Senate, debate on a typical bill has no time limit. Senators will sometimes filibuster (i.e. stall and prevent a bill from being brought to a vote) and at least 60 votes are required to overcome a filibuster. When a bill is considered under the rules of budget reconciliation, however, debate is limited to 20 hours and ending debate requires only a simple 51-vote majority.[76] Because of the vague wording in the budget act, reconciliation has been used several times by both Republicans and Democrats to push through legislation not necessarily related to the budget process.

Summary

The budgeting process is in some ways a good example of how the checks and balances in the American constitutional system limit the power of any one branch of government. The President initiates the process but it is Congress that ultimately implements the budget. The President may choose to veto certain legislation, but Congress may override the veto.

There are major problems with the current process. In FY2011, Congress failed to submit a budget resolution. This is inexcusable, given that FY2009 and FY2010 were to date the largest deficits in our history. More importantly, over 60% of spending is associated with so-called mandatory programs that need no explicit passage of legislation in order for funding to continue. Even if non-security discretionary spending is eliminated, we will continue, according to OMB estimates, to run deficits for the next 10 years. In some years (e.g., FY2009 and likely FY2011) **all** discretionary spending could be eliminated and we'd still have deficits. This leaves us with two options – increase revenues (via taxes), or pass laws making changes to the mandatory programs. I have already argued against higher taxes, and will argue this point again in Chapter 6 and 7. Mandatory spending must be addressed. Budgets with estimated surpluses must be required by law.

Chapter 6 – Cautionary Tales

—

"Think what you do when you run in debt; you give to another the power over your liberty."
– Benjamin Franklin

Introduction

If we can learn from history, we should study other countries who have succumbed to debt. Perhaps there are common patterns to recognize and hopefully avoid or undo in our future. Recently, in 2009 and 2010, the debt problems of Greece made international headlines[77]. But Greece is a small country mired in socialism; 40% of Greece's economy comes from its public sector[78], and its labor unions are vocal opponents of any entitlement reform[79]. Greece hasn't been a world superpower for over 2000 years.

Instead, it may be instructive to study larger and more powerful countries. I've chosen to analyze Argentina and Japan. Both of these countries had very large economies in recent history, and both suffered because of debt.

Argentina

The Founding Fathers of America believed free market principles could successfully be applied in other nations. Argentina is an example of that theory put into practice.

After declaring and then winning its independence from Spain in 1816, Argentina got off to a rocky start as a new nation[80]. An initial constitution was drawn up in 1826, but disputes between urban and rural residents eventually gave rise to a dictatorship under Juan Manuel de Rosas, who ruled from 1829-1852. After Rosas was overthrown by General Justo Jose de Urquiza, delegates from across the Argentinian provinces (with the key exception of Buenos Aires) met and drew up a constitution very similar to the United States. A confederation of provinces was established under this constitution.

In 1859, the confederation president Urquiza tried to force Buenos Aires to join the confederation. After a series of battles, Buenos Aires eventually agreed to enter the confederation in 1862. Argentina was now a country, and it enjoyed a stable government for nearly 70 years. Argentina's Presidents worked at attracting European immigrants and investments to grow the economy. Starting in the mid 1800's, a wave of immigrant settlers increased the population from 1 to nearly 8 million people by 1914. With its fertile farmlands and a modernized infrastructure (from foreign investments), Argentina built a large and export-led agricultural economy.

Argentina's economy continued to grow during and after World War I, with increasing exports of agricultural products to European countries. In the 1920's, Argentina ranked among the world's wealthiest nations. This would change as a result of the worldwide business slowdown from the Great Depression in 1929. Additionally, there were other factors already in place that would hurt Argentina.

During Argentina's rapid growth in the late 1800's, politics were dominated by wealthy conservatives who were able to prevent opposing candidates from winning elections. In 1889, the new Unión Cívica Radical party, which later became the Radical Party, formed and demanded election reform. By 1910, President Peña, a member of the conservative party, helped bring about election reform by providing for a secret ballot and requiring every man over 18 years of age to vote. In 1916, the Radical Party candidate Hipolito Irigoyen was elected President.

Despite a conservative majority in parliament, Irigoyen was able to pass social reforms, including a Labor Code establishing the right to strike, minimum wages, collective contracts (i.e. unions), and the first entirely state-run oil company in the world. The Radical Party remained in control until 1930, when Army leaders removed Irigoyen from power. This set the stage for several subsequent military dictatorships.

The most well-known leader during this time was Colonel Juan Perón, who rose to power while serving in various government positions under a series of army generals. Before assuming the presidency in 1946, Perón served as the head of the Department of Labor. This lead to an alliance with socialist and labor union leaders and helped increased the unions', the department's, and his own power. As minister of labor, Perón increased union worker wages, paid holidays, and other benefits. It was during this tenure Perón would meet, and later marry, radio star Eva Duarte.

Government spending greatly increased under the Perón presidency, and the government took over many of the nation's industries, while discouraging foreign investment. Taxes were levied against farm products, in an attempt to help manufacturing. This resulted in a drop in farm production and the nation's income. However, wages (under government/union direction) continued to rise. Perón also suspended freedom of speech and freedom of the press, and changed the Argentina constitution to increase his power and allow for a second term. Wikipedia summarizes Perón's tenure as follows,

> *During Perón's tenure, wages and working conditions improved appreciably, unionization was fostered, strategic industries and services were nationalized, import substitution industrialization and urban development were prioritized over the agrarian sector.*
>
> *Formerly stable prices and exchange rates were disrupted, however: the peso lost about 70% of its value from early 1948 to early 1950, and inflation reached 50% in 1951. Foreign policy became more isolationist, straining U.S.-Argentine relations. Perón intensified censorship as well as repression: 110 publications were shuttered, and numerous opposition figures were imprisoned and tortured. Advancing a personality cult, Perón rid himself of many important and capable advisers, while promoting patronage. A violent coup, which bombarded the Casa Rosada and its surroundings killing many, deposed him in 1955. He fled into exile, eventually residing in Spain.*

The World Book Encyclopedia summarizes the after effects,

> *Perón's attempt to strengthen manufacturing industries rapidly at the expense of the rural economy caused Argentina to suffer economically. Economic problems of large debts, high inflation, and little growth in productivity developed in the mid-1950's. However, support for Perón's policies continued, especially among labor unions.*

In 1956, military leaders took over the government and restored the Constitution of 1853. Arturo Frondizi assumed the presidency in 1958, and made attempts to cut government spending and reduce the debt. Economically, he signed laws that gave incentives and tax benefits to both local and foreign corporations willing to develop Argentina's energy and industry sectors. By the end of Frondizi's presidency, oil production tripled (nearly eliminating the need for imports), and refining capacity more than doubled. Automobile production more than tripled - again eliminating the need for imports.

Frondizi was opposed at times by both the people/unions (who disliked actions calling for financial sacrifice) and the military (who feared Frondizi would yield to pressure from the Perón supporters); he was removed from office by the military in 1962. Civilian presidents and military leaders would rule until 1972.

Argentina's economy worsened throughout the late 1960's and early 1970's, as did the stability of the government. Following a series of protests, strikes, and violence, the long exiled Juan Perón was actually able to return to the presidency in 1973. He died the following year, and his vice president and 3rd wife Isabel assumed the presidency. She was arrested in 1976 by military leaders who took control.

Instable governments, violence, and high inflation continued. A more recent analysis of Argentina and its economy can be found in the 2009 CIA World Fact Book,

> *Although one of the world's wealthiest countries 100 years ago, Argentina suffered during most of the 20th century from recurring economic crises, persistent fiscal and current account deficits, high inflation, mounting external debt, and capital flight. A severe depression, growing public and external indebtedness, and a bank run culminated in 2001 in the most serious economic, social, and political crisis in the country's turbulent history. Interim President Adolfo Rodriguez declared a default - the largest in history - on the government's foreign debt in December of that year, and abruptly resigned only a few days after taking office.*

Lesson from Argentina

There are parallels between the history of Argentina and the United States. Both countries had a weak initial constitution, and would eventually fight a series of battles to force all regions to join/remain part of the country. They both encouraged private investments and an influx of motivated immigrants to become among the wealthiest nations by the early 20th century.

During their formative years, Argentina and the United States did not have large entitlement programs in place. Immigrants were attracted by the opportunity (and freedom) to succeed. The national government played a role in encouraging, rather than controlling or running, industries. By the 20th century, both countries faced a rise in socialism that would threaten their form of government. It is at this point where there is a divergence in the fate and path of the two countries. Several factors played a role in the economic problems and eventual indebtedness of Argentina, including:

- Government corruption. Argentina's history is mired in corruption, violence, military coups, etc. Here in America, we are fortunate in that most of our internal debates, enactment of laws, and changes in leadership have happened peacefully. While a stable/peaceful society doesn't equate to a debt free society, it provides a better set of conditions for free markets and personal freedom.

- Nationalization of industry. Starting with President Irigoyen and expanding rapidly under Perón, Argentina's government took control of many industries. A government run company isn't necessarily efficient; profitability and positive cash-flow are not requirements. A lack of competition and the backing of the government can also result in damaging decisions. In the case of Argentina, the government taxed the successful (and private) agrarian part of its economy in an attempt to build up nationalized manufacturing companies. The results were disastrous for everyone.

- Entitlements. Large number of government employees (including those working in the nationalized companies), guaranteed wages/benefits, and government directed wage increases. These are all part of Argentina's history.

Japan

In August of 1945, a defeated Japan came under control of General Douglas MacArthur[81]. With many cities in ruins and an economy in shambles, Japan was a shadow of its formal world superpower status of the early 1900's. MacArthur and his advisors drafted a new constitution which went into effect on May 3rd, 1947. This constitution, which transferred ruling power from the emperor to the people, provided three branches of government – legislative, executive, and judicial. It also guaranteed certain rights, including the freedom of speech, of religion, of press, and of assembly.

Japan was able to return to pre-war production levels by the mid 1950's, and experienced an average 10% economic growth from 1960-1970. With a hardworking, well-trained work force, Japan imported technologies from the West and invested heavily in new plants and equipment. It also studied Western techniques (some of which were ignored by the West itself[82]) to improve the quality and demand for its products abroad. Japan also benefitted from a small defense allocation (1% of GDP)[83].

By the 1980's, it was the Western countries who were studying Japan to improve their own economies. In 1980, Japan was the 2nd largest economy in the world – second only to the United States. This is even more impressive when considering Japan is geographically a fraction of the size of the U.S. and, in 1980, half the number of citizens. From 1980 to 1995, Japan's economy grew from 38% to 71% as large as the United States'. Based on growth, Japan was on its way to becoming the world's largest economy.

Fast forward to 2010 – Japan is not the world's largest economy; it is the 3rd largest, having been surpassed by China. Japan's estimated 2010 debt as a percentage of GDP is 225%, the 2nd largest ratio of all 183 countries tracked by the International Monetary Fund World Economic Outlook Database[84]. Table 7-1 shows debt as a percentage of GDP among several countries since 1980. Japan's debt ratio is 95 percentage points higher than Greece, and 61 points higher than Argentina at its worst point (2002). Based on the data in table 7-1, you might think Japan is on the brink of an economic meltdown. Economist Yukio Noguchi, who correctly predicted a collapse in Japan's bubble economy in 1987, agrees. In a March 2010 article of The Japan Times, Noguchi stated Japan's public debt is likely to bankrupt the government and trigger catastrophic hyper-inflation. "There is little hope," Noguchi stated. "Japan's fiscal conditions are so bad, it can no longer be fixed without causing inflation. I'm very pessimistic."[85]

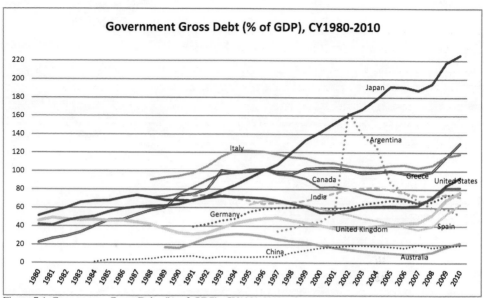

Figure 7-1 Government Gross Debt (% of GDP), CY1980-2010. Source: International Monetary Fund World Economic Outlook Database, October 2010 Edition

To be fair, Japan has a few things going for it. For one, Japan has a considerable amount of assets (e.g., Japan is the 2nd largest holder of U.S. public debt, as discussed in Chapter 2) to offset some of its debt. Also, 95% of Japan's debt is domestically owned, and yields on Japanese Government Bonds (JGB) have been effectively fixed at 1.3% (compared to 3.6% yields on U.S. Treasury bonds)[86]. This means Japan is able to finance its debt more cheaply than other countries. However, IMF projections indicate Japan will need to tap into foreign markets as early as 2019, and foreign investors will likely demand a higher rate of return[87]. Japan also has an aging population (more so than the United States) and declining birthrate, meaning its Social Security program may be a ticking time bomb.

Table 7-2 show "net debt" (gross debt minus financial assets) as a percentage of GDP. Net debt information isn't available for all of the countries in Table 7-1 (and some countries, like China, have no net debt), but I've included several countries for comparative purposes. Considering net debt, Japan is worse off than even Greece.

I also included GDP for Japan and the United States in figure 7-2. Notice how Japan's GDP starts to fall after 1995 (as its net debt continues to increase); in this year, the U.S. GDP continues to rise as its net debt decreases.

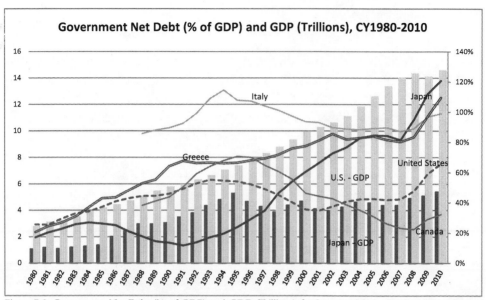

Figure 7-2, Government Net Debt (% of GDP) and GDP (Trillions) for Japan and U.S., CY1980-2010. Source: International Monetary Fund World Economic Outlook Database, October 2010 Edition

Lesson from Japan

Japan is in bad shape; how did this happen? From 1980-2010, Japan's revenue as a percentage of GDP has been relatively stable, but its expenses have exceeded revenue for all but six years (1987-1992). Its economy has also stagnated for nearly two decades. I've identified three key factors contributing to Japan's increasing debt and poor economy.

- Stimulus programs. Similar to recent events in the United States, Japan experienced a recession in the early 1990's from a bursting of its real estate and stock market bubbles.[88] Japan responded with stimulus spending. The failure of these efforts was evident by 2001. In his article, "Lessons on How NOT to Stimulate the Economy"[89], Ronal Utt remarked,

    Beginning in 1991-1992, Japan adopted the spending approach now advocated by many in the U.S. Congress when it embarked on a massive nationwide program of infrastructure investment. Between 1992 and 2000, Japan implemented 10 separate spending stimulus packages in which public infrastructure investment was a major component.

The results were bad for Japan's debt and, Utt noted, its economy and citizens,

> *Combined with increases in other government spending programs, Japan's efforts to spend its way to prosperity led to substantial increases in government spending as a share of GDP. ... Japan's failed policies had severe negative consequences for its economy and citizens. ...[M]easured in inflation-adjusted GDP growth, Japan went from being a high-growth country in the 1980s to a slow-growth country during the 1990s. ... For the average Japanese citizen, the chief consequence of this economic underperformance has been both a relative and an absolute decline in the nation's standard of living.*

Japan decided to double down on government stimulus spending in the 2000's. A February 2009 New York Times article noted,

> *Japan's rural areas have been paved over and filled in with roads, dams and other big infrastructure projects, the legacy of trillions of dollars spent to lift the economy from a severe downturn caused by the bursting of a real estate bubble in the late 1980s. During those nearly two decades, Japan accumulated the largest public debt in the developed world — totaling 180 percent of its $5.5 trillion economy — while failing to generate a convincing recovery.*

- Economic "engineering" on the part of the government. When Japan's economy tanked in the early 1990's, the banks held a considerable amount of bad debt. Rather than recognizing their losses, banks were encouraged to keep lending money to failing companies. Anil K. Kashyap wrote in 1996[90],

> *Many banks continued to extend credit to insolvent borrowers, gambling that these firms would recover or that the government would bail them out. The Japanese government also encouraged banks to increase their lending to small- and medium-sized firms to ease the credit crunch after 1998.*

Kashyap called this practice "Zombie Lending" in which banks lend to "zombie firms". As of October 2009, the Japanese government has decided to greatly expand these policies.[91]

Let me suggest the Japanese government was not merely misguided in its efforts to revive the economy. Increasing debts, patronage, and collusion drive destructive behavior. As Charles Smith noted in 2001[92],

> *But there are deeper political problems in the Japanese system. Rural populations carries more political weight in the Diet [Japanese legislative branch] than their numbers alone*

would dictate, creating an expensive patronage system of rural subsidies as politicians curry favor with farmers and maintain rural employment with pork-barrel spending.

And the intricate, collusive game of musical chairs between government and corporate debt--the bankrupt insurance companies own a ton of government bonds, which were sold to fund low-cost loans to failing companies, which can't be allowed to go belly up because the bonds would have to be written off--form a sclerotic mass in the body politic. The greatest resistance, however, may come from the "doken kokka," the so-called "construction state" of lenders, builders and politicians which feeds off the massive and mostly useless public works funded by the deficits. This "construction-industrial complex" employs six million workers and consumes 20% of the GDP, perhaps the greatest and most politically potent "make work" project since the Great Pyramids.

In short, there are powerful interests who benefit from the current stasis.

- Increased Taxes. Increasing taxes is not a spending problem – but it can stunt an economy and actually result in lower overall revenues. And if expenses rise independent of the economy (e.g., Social Security, welfare), higher taxes may result in more debt. As Japan's stimulus programs failed to provide any boost to the economy, and debts continued to mount, Japan responded with a series of additional and increased taxes.[93] In a 1998 article, the CATO institute noted,

    From 1989 to 1992, Japan added more taxes on sales, land, capital gains, dividends and interest. Yet the dramatic deterioration in economic growth after 1990 is rarely blamed, even in part, on those simultaneous changes in tax policy. The sole exception was the increased VAT of April 1997. Even in that case, however, complaints that this particular tax increase hurt the economy are not often translated into the logical conclusion that rolling-back such a counterproductive tax increase must likewise help the economy.

Increased taxes did not help decrease the debt - and they did not result in additional tax revenues. Revenue as a percentage of GDP in 1995 was no higher than the 1980 level despite *"15 years of bracket creep, a new VAT, and new taxes on interest income, capital gains, and land."*[94] Instead, the tax increases stunted economic growth. It is interesting to note tax increases had actually begun to slow down the Japanese economy prior to the 1990's,

Before 1975, tax policy greatly reduced effective marginal tax rates and eased the multiple taxation of saved income. Economic growth in Japan ... averaged 9.6% a year from 1952 to 1973.

From 1975 to 1987, "bracket creep" and higher Social Security taxes reversed much of the previous progress on marginal tax rates. Economic growth slowed to 4.3% from 1975 to 1991[95].

Will we learn from History?

Argentina's history shows how socialism ruins an economy and drives up debt. The more recent events in Japan are a cautionary tale to government economic engineering and stimulus spending. With both countries, it was the response to problems that defined their future. Unfortunately, the free market principles that help a country become prosperous are sometimes abandoned when hard times come along.

When analyzing Japan's decisions in the 1990's, it is hard not to become angry with the United States government. Japan experienced a crisis similar to what the U.S. began facing in 2008. America had a clear and very recent model of what **not** to do in terms of reviving an economy and avoiding debt – and yet we followed right in Japan's footsteps. It started with President George Bush Jr. He initially tried stimulus spending in the form of tax rebates during the 2001 recession, which were ineffective; the economy didn't recovery until tax rate reductions were introduced two years later.[96] In 2008, with America's economy showing signs of trouble, Congress passed and President Bush signed into law stimulus efforts such as:

- the Economic Stimulus Act (a $168 billion program[97] with $94 billion spent through FY2009, according to the 2009 Financial Report of the United States Government)
- the Housing and Economic Recovery Act (a $300 billion program[98] with $187 billion spent or recognized as liabilities through FY2009, according to the 2009 Financial Report of the United States Government)
- the Troubled Asset Relief Program (a $700 billion program[99] with $383 billion spent through FY2009, according to the 2009 Financial Report of the United States Government)

The spending continued with President Obama. In February 2009, as his stimulus bill (the American Recovery and Reinvestment Act, ARRA) was working its way through Congress, a group of economists argued,

> *Japan's approach failed to accomplish more not because of waste but because it was never tried wholeheartedly … instead of making one big push to pump up the economy with economic shock therapy, Japan spread its spending out over several years, diluting the effects.* "[100]

The stimulus bill passed and the U.S. had its "shock therapy"; the economists were wrong. President Obama's $787 billion ARRA of 2009 was intended to "combat… the worst economic crisis since the Great Depression" and keep the unemployment rate below 8 percent by "saving or creating 3.5 million jobs" [101]. In November of 2009, unemployment exceeded 10 percent. The economy shrunk by 2% in 2009 (the first annual decline in 50 years) and the U.S. recorded its largest deficit ($1.4 trillion) ever. The FY2010 deficit came in at $1.3 trillion[102] (the 2nd largest ever) and November 2010 unemployment was at 9.8%.

Summary

How do you drive up debt and ruin an economy in the process? Here are five proven tactics:

- engage in economic engineering
- introduce entitlement programs
- implement socialism, specifically nationalization of key industries
- respond to financial recessions with government stimulus spending
- as debt rises, increase taxes rather than reduce spending

For completeness sake, let's add a 6th tactic to the list:

- attempt to monetize the debt (note - monetize the debt is a fancy term for printing money; this happened in Argentina, and was a contributor to its inflationary problems in the 1980's[103])

The decline of Argentina and Japan are illustrative, but we don't even have to look at other countries to learn from history. The United States, in the not too distant past, made poor decisions that affect us today. In February 2009, the same economists promoting stimulus spending for the United States argued Japan's stimulus efforts helped save its economy from "an outright 1930s-style collapse".[104] But a careful study of history indicates the Great Depression was actually caused by economic engineering and prolonged by stimulus spending.

There are startling parallels between the federal government's decisions in the 1930's and its recent handling of the 2008 recession. I'll cover this in the next chapter, but let me briefly summarize the Great Depression. Referring back to figure 3-3 in Chapter 3, federal expenses increased by over 275% from 1930-1939. Table 1-1 in Chapter 1 indicates the debt increased by 250%. What was the result of all of this government spending and debt? GDP in 1940 was still lower than 1929 levels; unemployment was still higher. According to a 2004 study by UCLA economists Harold Cole and Lee Ohanian, the Great Depression was extended by seven years due to "ill-conceived stimulus policies"[105]. And lastly, America was given an entitlement program (Social Security) with a present day (FY2009) debt obligation of over $7 trillion (refer to Table 4-4 in Chapter 4) that then paved the way for an additional entitlement program (Medicare, passed by President LBJ in 1965 and then expanded under President Bush in 2003) with a debt obligation of over $38 trillion.

Chapter 7 – Where are we Headed?

—

"We have tried spending money. We are spending more than we have ever spent before and it does not work. ... We have never made good on our promises. ... I say after eight years of this Administration we have just as much unemployment as when we started ... and an enormous debt to boot!" – Henry Morgenthau, Treasury Secretary under FDR

Introduction

We are headed for a train wreck, and the train has been building speed for many years. Chart after chart in this book shows the debt increasing at an exponential rate from the mid 2000's onward (if you've jumped straight to this chapter, go back and look at figure 1-1, 1-2, or 2-7). From Chapter 4, the actual debt of the U.S. government at the end of FY2009 is $57 trillion dollars. 80% of this amount comes from the net present value obligations of Social Security and Medicare. These programs, along with other entitlements identified in Chapter 3, are resulting in increasingly large annual deficits. These deficits, in turn, require increasingly large interest payments to service the debt.

Current Policies are not sustainable

In its 2009 Financial Report, the U.S. Government identifies the problems in the future rate of spending. Figure 7-1, taken from the Citizen's Guide section of the report, charts estimated receipts and program spending (less interest payments) as a percentage of GDP for the next seventy years; figure 7-2 adds in the interest payments. As the guide points out,

> *Program spending grew rapidly in 2008 and 2009 due to the financial crisis and the recession and the policies necessary to combat both, and is expected to fall in the next few years as the economy recovers. Starting in 2014, however, rising health care costs and, to a lesser extent, the aging population, are expected to cause program spending as a share of GDP to rise continuously from 19 percent in 2014 to 25 percent in 2040 and 29 percent in 2080.*

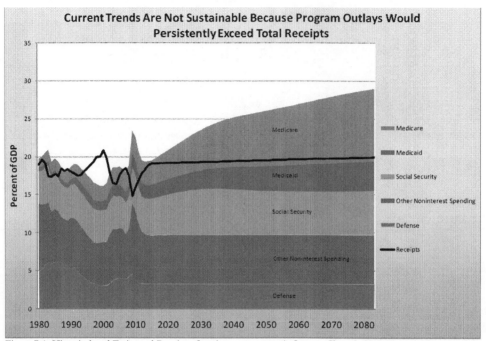

Figure 7-1, Historical and Estimated Receipts (less interest payment), Source: Chart 8, 2009 Financial Report of the United States Government.

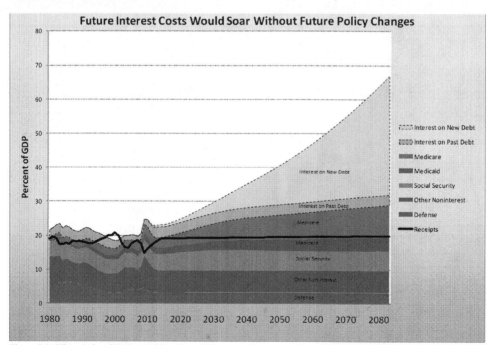

Figure 7-2, Historical and Estimated Receipts with Interest payments, Source: Chart 9, 2009 Financial Report of the United States Government

That's an alarming prediction – which may actually be optimistic. In figures 7-1/7-2, there is the assumption that 1) receipts quickly rise and stay at pre FY2008 levels, and 2) government spending quickly falls from its FY2009 level.

As I mentioned at the end of Chapter 4, the government in its 2010 Financial Report makes an assumption the ACA will dramatically reduce Medicare costs and not be a significant cost burden itself. With this in mind, they have adjusted their estimates on future outlays and expenses (figure 7-3). Even with these unrealistic assumptions, the government expects continual deficits.

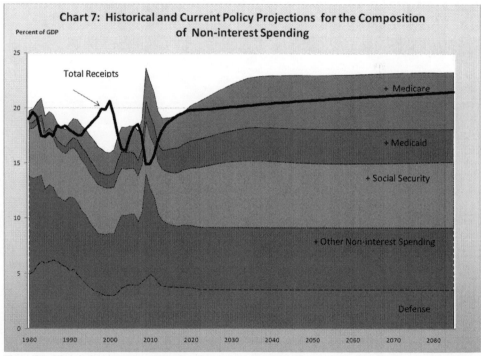

Figure 7-3, Historical and Estimated Receipts (less interest payment), Source: 2010 Financial Report of the United States Government.

Using the estimated deficits and factoring in interest payments, the 2010 Financial Report extrapolates the debt held by the public as a percentage of GDP (figure 7-4). Again, the 2009 projection line is without the assumption of savings from the ACA. By 2030, the ratio will exceed the previous high during World War II and will then continue to rise at an exponential rate. Note figure 7-4 doesn't include the intragovernmental holdings component of the debt (refer back to Chapter 2) so most of the historical ratios seem lower than the **total debt** ratios we've typically discussed. But, because the underlying obligations of the intragovernmental holdings manifest themselves in future deficits, which are then reflected in the debt held by the public, this chart is an accurate way of estimating the future debt.

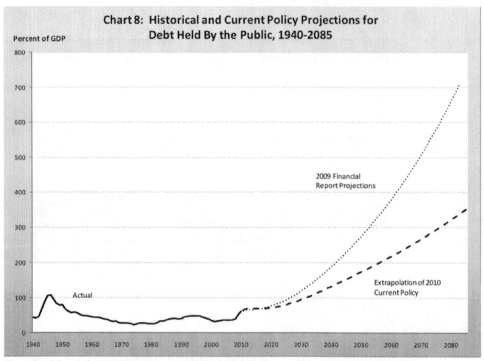

Figure 7-4, Historical and Estimated Debt Held By the Public, Source: Chart 2, 2010 Financial Report of the United States Government

As the 2009 financial report concludes,

> *These estimates illustrate that current policies are not sustainable....The nation must change course and bring social insurance expenses and resources in balance before the deficit and debt reach unprecedented heights. Delays will only increase the magnitude of the reforms needed and will place more of the burden on future generations.*

The 2010 financial report purports a partial "solution,"

> *The United States took a potentially significant step towards fiscal sustainability in 2010 by enacting the ACA. The legislated changes for Medicare, Medicaid, and other parts of the health care system hold the prospect of lowering the long-term growth trend for health care costs and significantly reducing the long-term fiscal gap.*

I believe the "prospect of lowering the long-term growth trend" is slim to none. In fact, I believe the current government is making matters worse on a number of fronts.

Stimulus spending and big government

Prior to 1930, the U.S. government did not respond to financial recessions with increased spending. The Great Depression marked a dramatic change in the role of the federal government. To illustrate, I've extracted the five major depressions and financial panics along with the Great Depression in figure 7-5. I've also included the 2008 Recession, using data available through October 2010.

Note – the start and end date for each event comes from the National Bureau of Economic Research (NBER)[106]. The NBER identifies a recession/depression and its duration by analyzing several factors such as GDP, real income, unemployment rates, industrial production, and wholesale-retail sales. Many textbooks and historians consider the Great Depression to have ended in 1940-41. I will use the official 3.7 year duration from the NBER for analysis (the NBER identifies a separate recession that took place from 1937-1938) but will also consider the decade-long duration when drawing conclusions.

Event	Date	Years	Avg. Unemp- loyment	Debt (% GDP) Begin	End	5 Year Recovery Avg. GDP Growth	Avg. Unemp- loyment
Depression-1815	03/23/1815 12/31/1820	5.8		10.9%	12.3%	-24.3%	
Depression-1840	01/01/1840 12/31/1843	4.0		0.2%	2.1%	44.9%	
Panic of 1873	10/01/1873 03/01/1879	5.4		27.2%	28.0%	49.5%	
Panic of 1893, 1896	01/01/1893 06/30/1897	4.5	14.5%	9.4%	11.7%	33.8%	3.7%
Depresion-1920	08/01/1920 07/31/1921	1.6	8.5%	36.1%	27.1%	19.5%	1.8%
Great Depression	08/01/1929 03/31/1933	3.7	18.3%	17.4%	38.4%	-5.7%	14.3%
Recession-2008	12/31/2007 06/30/2009	1.5	6.8%	63.6%	82.3%	3.8%	9.7%

Figure 7-5 Five major depressions/financial panics, along with the Great Depression and 2008 Recession. Source: U.S. Treasury Bureau of Public Debt, U.S. Bureau of Economic Analysis (GDP), Bureau of Labor Statistics & U.S. Bureau of the Census (unemployment), http://en.wikipedia.org/wiki/List_of_recessions_in_the_United_States (event timelines)

The Great Depression stands alone from its predecessors. The debt, as a percentage of GDP, increased 21 percentage points; the panic of 1893/1896, the closest runner up, increased the ratio by just 2 percentage points. Referring back to figure 3-3 in Chapter 3, the increase in debt during the Great Depression was driven by spending; annual outlays in 1933 where 47% higher than they were in 1929. Other than the Depression of 1815, the Great Depression is also unique in terms of the subsequent economic recovery. For the five years after it ended, average annual GDP growth was -5.7%; unemployment averaged 14.3%. Figure 7-5 makes a strong argument that stimulus spending isn't necessary to combat a financial depression, and that it actually hurts economic recovery.

History may be repeating itself. During the 2008 Recession, debt as a percentage of GDP increased 18 percentage points – nearly as much as the increase during the Great Depression, but in just half the time. Considering factors such as unemployment, the "recovery" from the 2008 Recession doesn't seem much like a recovery at all. With a rapid increase in debt, there is a very real risk of an anemic economy and high unemployment for years to come, along with another recession. The debt from entitlement programs often hurts a future generation, but the debt from stimulus spending and big government can hurt the current generation.

Another Great Depression?

The similarities between the Great Depression and the 2008 Recession are easier to understand when considering each event in terms of three phases.

Phase 1 – Economic crisis caused by the government

During the 1920's, government monetary and credit policy (via the Federal Reserve) artificially heated up the economy. Subsequent attempts in 1928/1929 to stave off inflation resulted in a drastic decrease in the money supply along with a drop in investor and business confidence. The 1929 stock market crash was a reflection of policies and not the direct cause of the Great Depression (**note** - see the appendix for more details on the causes and events of the Great Depression).

As the major cause of the 2008 Recession, the housing crisis can be directly attributed to government economic engineering. Similar to the Great Depression, many people have attempted to place blame for the 2008 Recession on the financial market and it participants. Some would have us believe "Irresponsible risk-taking and debt-fueled speculation – unchecked by sound oversight – led to the near-collapse of our financial system."[107] But as Darrell Issa noted in the U.S. House of Representatives report "The Role of Government Affordable Housing Policy in Creating the Global Financial Crisis of 2008,"[108]

> *The housing bubble that burst in 2007 ... can be traced back to federal government intervention in the U.S. housing market intended to help provide homeownership opportunities for more Americans. This intervention began with two government-backed corporations, Fannie Mae and Freddie Mac, which privatized their profits but socialized their risks, creating powerful incentives for them to act recklessly and exposing taxpayers to tremendous losses. Government intervention also created "affordable" but dangerous lending policies which encouraged lower down payments, looser underwriting standards and higher leverage. Finally, government intervention created a nexus of vested interests – politicians, lenders and lobbyists – who profited from the "affordable" housing market and acted to kill reforms.*

As author Mark Levin noted, the Federal Reserve also played a role in the housing crisis[109] - very much like its role during the Great Depression. From January 2001 to June 2003, interest rates were reduced from 6.5 to 1.0 percent, increasing the money and credit supply, and helping the entitlement lending goals of the government. Then, fearing inflation, rates were raised from 1.0 to 5.25 percent from June 2004 to June 2005 thereby decreasing the money supply, and setting up a nice surprise for most of the low income home owners who financed with adjustable rate mortgages. This manipulation of interest rates increased and then decreased the money supply – destabilizing the economy by interfering with normal market conditions.

Phase 2 – A failure in conservatism

While considered by many to be a conservative free-market politician, President Hoover (president from 1929-1933) implemented a number of destructive policies including:

- The Smoot-Hawley Tariff law (1930), which severely limited importation of foreign produce and goods and ignited an international trade war resulting in a massive failure among farmers and banks. Federal spending increased greatly in 1930 and 1931, with hundreds of millions paid in subsidies to affected domestic farmers.

- The Revenue Act (1932), which doubled the income tax rate, and more than doubled the top income bracket, from 24 to 63 percent. The act increased corporate and estate taxes, imposed new taxes on gasoline, gifts, and automobiles, lowered exemptions, and did away with the earned income credit.

- The formation of the Reconstruction Finance Corporation (1932), which provided billions in business subsidies. This was on top of the hundreds of millions paid to farmers adversely affected by Smoot-Hawley.

Hoover created a debt blueprint for his successor. Rexford Tugwell, an architect of FDR's policies in the 1930's, would later say "We didn't admit it at the time, but practically the whole New Deal was extrapolated from programs that Hoover started."[110]

In December, 2008, Republican President Bush Jr. told CNN Television "I've abandoned free-market principles to save the free-market system ... to make sure the economy doesn't collapse."[111] As discussed in the last chapter, President Bush passed over a trillion dollars in stimulus spending in 2008, paving the way for President Obama and the Democratic controlled Congress to run up the largest deficits in history. It should also be noted President Bush greatly increased the scope of Medicare with the passage of the prescription drug benefit in 2003[112]

(Medicare Part D). Over budget as soon as it was passed[113], this new benefit has a present value (FY 2009) debt obligation of $7 trillion.

Phase 3 – Big government "to the rescue"

Though campaigning on a platform to reverse the "reckless and extravagant" spending of Hoover, FDR continued with the status quo of big government. Blaming the Depression on "unscrupulous money changers,"[114] FDR seized the country's private gold holdings, ended Prohibition, and increased government expenditures by 79% between 1933 and 1936. He convinced Congress to create Social Security (1935) and passed some of the most radical laws to date[115] including:

- The National Industrial Recovery Act (NIRA) in 1933, which forced most manufacturing industries into government cartels with over 500 codes dictating pricing, means of production, and terms of sale. While this law was eventually deemed unconstitutional, it stunted the economy (e.g., industrial production dropped 25% in just six months after the law went into effect) and hurt investor confidence.

- Several rounds of tax rate increases, culminating in a top income tax rate of 90%. FDR proposed a marginal tax rate of 99.5% for incomes over $100k and after this proposal failed, issued an executive order to tax income over $25k at 100%! Congress rescinded this order.

- The Civil Works Administration (CWA) in 1933. Originally created as a short-term jobs program, it was replaced by the Works Progress Administration (WPA) in 1935. The model of inefficiency (critics called it "We Piddle Around"), by 1941 "only 59 percent of the WPA budget went to paying workers anything at all; the rest was sucked up in administration and overhead."

- The National Labor Relations Act in 1935 (aka the Wagner Act), which moved labor disputes out of courts and into a new federal agency. This act was primarily aimed at "crushing all employer resistance to labor unions." Labor union memberships soared as a result, with 2.5 times as many members by 1941. Empowered labor unions went on a "militant organizing frenzy" with boycotts, strikes, and widespread violence that pushed productivity down and unemployment up.

With a campaign promise of change, President Obama picked up right where President Bush left off, albeit with more vigor and impact. Having increased the debt $3.2 trillion in his first 18 months alone (it took President Bush 4.3 years to do so), he is also repeating steps taken by FDR. Examples include:

- The American Recovery and Reinvestment Act (ARRA) of February 2009. This $787 billion stimulus package has failed to live up to the promise of keeping unemployment below 8% (unemployment averaged 9.6% in 2010). As of December 04, 2010, 73% of funds have spent across the following categories[116]

Category	Funds Paid Out (Billions)
Tax Benefits	$243.4
Contracts, Grants, Loans	$164.0
Entitlements	$173.0

Before ARRA passed, President Obama touted the availability of "shovel ready" infrastructure projects (e.g., road, bridge and sewer projects) that could benefit from stimulus spending. In an October 2010 interview, while acknowledging the projects took longer than anticipated to begin, the president maintained they would help the economy.[117] In his interview, the president said the benefit of infrastructure spending was that for every dollar spent, "you get a dollar and a half in stimulus because there are ripple effects from building roads or bridges or sewer lines." This is a fallacy, as shown by FDR's programs and Japan's recent efforts. Entitlement spending and redistributive tax benefits also do nothing to stimulate the economy.

- The Affordable Care Act (ACA) of 2010. In terms of potential debt, this program, according to the CBO, is expected to cost well over $2 trillion[118]. Much higher than the $940 billion touted by Congress during its passage, the major components of the program start in 2014. By looking at costs from this point on, Jeffrey Anderson from the Weekly Standard estimates net costs in the first decade to be somewhere between $2.5 and $3 trillion. And given the government's poor track record of estimating costs (e.g., Medicare – both at is onset and then again with Part D coverage), the actual costs are likely much higher.

- Fostering of unions. Union membership in the private sector has been on the decline for years, while membership in the public sector has steadily increased. In 2009, public employees became the majority of union members for the first time ever[119]. This phenomenon is not attributable to President Obama but, like FDR, he has a very favorable view towards unions. Even prior to his election, President Obama was promising his support for unionization to federal agencies like the TSA[120]. More recently, in the private sector, he helped the United Auto Workers health care trust fund gain significant ownership stakes in the reorganized General Motors (40%) and Chrysler (50%) companies[121]. Ironically it is the health care costs, pensions, and work rules of the unions that helped drive GM and Chrysler into bankruptcy[122].

- Tax increases. One of the most significant new taxes (but not yet passed as of Dec. 2010) favored by President Obama is typically referred to as cap-and-trade. A means of limiting the supposedly harmful greenhouse gases, the legislation limits ("caps") the amount of carbon a business may emit, unless they want to buy ("trade") credits for additional emissions. This bill could generate $646 billion in new taxes each year[123], but much of these taxes will ultimately be borne by the energy consumers. How much would this new legislation cost? An initial CBO report estimates an increase of $175 per year for each family[124] (this is an average cost, with non-trivial redistributive implications). Peter Orszag, the former OMB Director, put the estimate quite a bit higher – an additional $1300 in annual electricity costs[125]. Other analyses paint a much grimmer picture, primarily because the CBO estimate does not "take into account economic damage (lost jobs and a smaller economy) from higher energy prices."[126] The National Black Chamber of Commerce (NBCC) predicted 2.3 – 2.7 million fewer jobs[127], consistent with the Heritage Foundation estimate of 2.5 million[128]. In terms of debt potential, the Heritage Foundation finds "The overall gross domestic product losses will average $491 billion per year from 2012-2035 and the cumulative GDP loss is $9.4 trillion by 2035. This equates to a 26% increase in the national debt by 2035, an additional $115,000 per family[129]."

Summary

Will we have another depression? Is this the beginning of the United States' lost decade? I hope not – but I'll end this chapter with figure 7-6a and 7-6b aligned side-by-side and let you draw your own conclusion. The very real danger is that, like the Great Depression, big government spending will choke off economic recovery and result in a secondary recession, perhaps somewhere around 2013.

The U.S. government is engaging in all six tactics that drive up debt and ruin an economy – economic engineering, entitlement programs, socialism, stimulus spending, increased taxes, and, yes, even some monetization of the debt. It isn't called monetization of the debt though; instead, it is referred to as quantitative easing (QE). The Federal Reserve has already implemented two rounds of QE[130], once in 2008 and then again in 2010.

Even without the stimulus spending and socialistic slant of the current U.S. government, the annual costs of entitlement programs are skyrocketing. In current business jargon, we're seeing "hockey stick" growth. Or, taking a term from futurist Ray Kurzweil, we've hit the "knee of the curve."[131] While Kurzweil often talks about exponential growth in terms of useful scenarios, such as the doubling of computer processing power every 2-3 years, an exponentially rising debt is not beneficial.

World War II and with it, the revival of trade among allies, helped the U.S. out of the Great Depression. What can help the United States in the 21st century? There is one encouraging possibility. In late 2010, a new group of politicians was able to gain control in the U.S. House of Representatives[132]. With conservative principles and a rally around fighting excessive government spending and taxation[133], the Tea Party movement may be the beginning of a slow but necessary return to fiscal responsibility. But these new leaders must start talking about painful and traditionally unpopular topics if we hope to make any real dent in the debt.

This Page Is Intentionally Blank

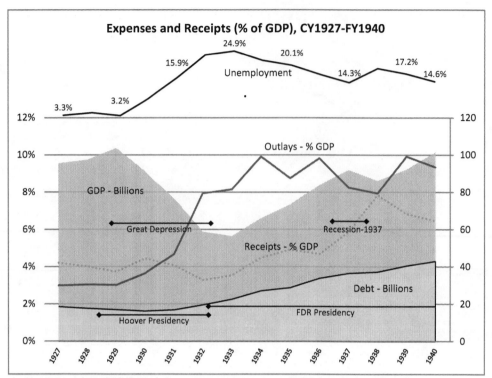

Figure 7-6a, Outlays (Expenses) and Receipts (% of GDP) for CY1927-1940. Source: U.S. Treasury Bureau of Public Debt, U.S. Bureau of Economic Analysis (GDP), Bureau of Labor Statistics & U.S. Bureau of the Census (unemployment), http://en.wikipedia.org/wiki/List_of_recessions_in_the_United_States (event timelines)

billions	1927	1928	1929	1930	1931	1932	1933	1934	1935	1936	1937	1938	1939	1940
Receipts	$4.01	$3.90	$3.86	$4.06	$3.12	$1.92	$2.00	$2.96	$3.61	$3.92	$5.39	$6.75	$6.30	$6.55
Outlays	$2.86	$2.96	$3.13	$3.32	$3.58	$4.66	$4.60	$6.54	$6.41	$8.23	$7.58	$6.84	$9.14	$9.47
Deficit	$1.16	$0.94	$0.74	$0.74	($0.46)	($2.74)	($2.60)	($3.59)	($2.80)	($4.31)	($2.19)	($0.09)	($2.85)	($2.92)
Debt	$18.51	$17.60	$16.93	$16.19	$16.80	$19.49	$22.54	$27.05	$28.70	$33.78	$36.42	$37.16	$40.44	$42.97

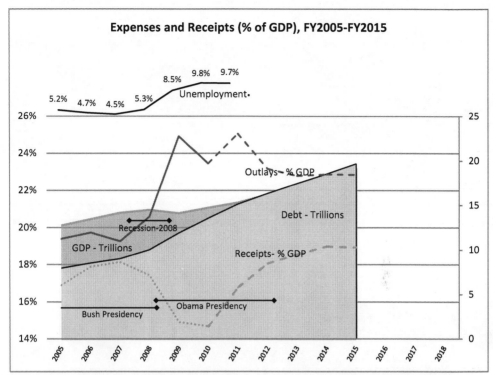

Figure 7-6b, Outlays (Expenses) and Receipts (% of GDP) for FY2005-2015. Source: U.S. Treasury Bureau of Public Debt, U.S. Bureau of Economic Analysis (GDP), Bureau of Labor Statistics & U.S. Bureau of the Census (unemployment), http://en.wikipedia.org/wiki/List_of_recessions_in_the_United_States (event timelines)

billions	2005	2006	2007	2008	2009	2010	2011e	2012e	2013e	2014e	2015e
Receipts	$2,154	$2,407	$2,568	$2,524	$2,105	$2,162	$2,567	$2,926	$3,188	$3,455	$3,634
Outlays	$2,472	$2,655	$2,729	$2,983	$3,518	$3,456	$3,834	$3,755	$3,915	$4,161	$4,386
Deficit	($318)	($248)	($161)	($459)	($1,413)	($1,294)	($1,267)	($828)	($727)	($706)	($752)
Debt	$7,933	$8,507	$9,008	$10,025	$11,910	$13,562	$15,144	$16,336	$17,453	$18,532	$19,683

Chapter 8 – Becoming Debt Free

—

For the Lord your God will bless you as He has promised you, and you will lend to many nations,
but you will not borrow; and you will rule over many nations, but they will not rule over you.
– Deuteronomy 15:6

Introduction

Few people are talking about the real changes needed to become debt free. Eliminating the debt is not complex; we need to aggressively attack the largest problem areas and generate surpluses from this point forward. The suggestions in this chapter may seem unrealistic; I believe they are straightforward and necessary. The alternative is to become a second-rate country mired in debt and mediocrity.

The United States didn't become a world superpower by providing entitlements and "equal things" to our citizenry. Our founding principles of limited government, free market economics, and individual responsibility may seem to some unfair and uncaring. But it is interesting to note that the poorest of our poor are still the envy of much of the world[134]. Did you know, as of 2005, over half of the world lives on less than the internationally defined poverty line of $2 a day[135]? By comparison, the U.S. Poverty level is $27.83[136] a day, and less than 13% of the U.S. population lives below this level[137]. We have a smaller percentage of poor people – and our poor are rich by world standards! That is a fact worth repeating. Think about the poor in the United States. How many of them have running water, access to food, and shelter? By world standards, our poor are rich.

Multiple support levels already in place

We should also remember there are already multiple levels of support to help citizens in times of need[138] – none of which involve the federal government.

1. Individual
   Every citizen should strive for self-sufficiency by saving for short and long-term needs, and by insuring against unforeseen losses. The free market is the best means of providing this insurance – be it life, property, health, disability, etc.

2. Family

A society without strong families is a society headed toward poverty and tyranny. Families are a vital support structure; we should all look to assist our immediate and extended families when needed. The apostle Paul stated quite plainly, "But if anyone does not provide for his relatives, and especially for members of his household, he has denied the faith and is worse than an unbeliever."[139] Realize that the perceived lack of family security was used by President Franklin Roosevelt when arguing for Social Security. He stated:

> [Economic] security was attained in the earlier days through the interdependence of members of families upon each other and of the families within a small community upon each other. The complexities of great communities and of organized industry make less real these simple means of security. Therefore, we are compelled to employ the active interest of the Nation as a whole through government in order to encourage a greater security for each individual who composes it.[140]

3. Church

For those without relatives willing and/or able to help, the church should provide members with short-term assistance.

4. Community

There are thousands of non-profit organizations designed to provide assistance to the poor and those temporarily in need.

5. Local government

6. State government

While not as ideal as options 1-4, local and state governments can provide temporary assistance to its own citizens.

An Entitlement is Legalized Stealing

Many people feel it is immoral to not help the poor and needy; I agree with them. Some people think the poor should have access to food, clothing, shelter, and even healthcare; I agree with them as well. But do we have a right to these things? Should the government play a role in ensuring and providing these "rights"?

If I decide to donate my car to a less fortunate neighbor, it is called charity. If I decide to donate my friend's car to a less fortunate neighbor, it is called stealing. When the government takes from one person to give to another, it is also stealing. It doesn't matter how noble or well intentioned the motives, entitlement programs are a form of legalized stealing. Entitlement programs are immoral.

God loves a cheerful giver, and I believe many Americans are quite willing to help others. But coerced giving is much different than doing so voluntarily. For one thing, volunteer giving can be done on as-needed basis, and it doesn't create a sense of entitlement on behalf of the receiver. Volunteer giving is not immoral.

You may or may not agree with me. If not, hopefully you agree we cannot afford our existing entitlement programs; certainly, we cannot afford to add new ones. We need to make major changes. Let me propose a 7-point plan to eliminate the debt.

1.   Restate the national debt, eliminate Trust Funds

It is difficult to fix what can't be measured. As discussed in Chapter 4, the actual total debt is much worse than the number provided by the Treasury Department. We need to eliminate the notion of Trust Funds and Government Account Securities; they are deceitful (i.e. there are no funds in the trust fund), they do not track actual liabilities, and they earn no actual interest. Let's restate the debt based on the net present values of all underlying liabilities, with the goal of phasing out all such liabilities.

2.   Phase out Social Security

As we've discussed in Chapter 2, Social Security is a deceitful program. Let me also state it is inefficient and unnecessary. According to a study by the Heritage Foundation, Social Security has historically provided a 1.23% or less return on investment[141]. By way of comparison, an individual could earn a return of over 5% by investing in an equal mix of Treasury bills and stocks. In their example, a two-income family would end up with $450,000 in benefits under Social Security as opposed to $975,000 under private investments.

Social Security is also inefficient for the government, who must pay for all interest accrued. The various Social Security trust funds are comprised of Government

Account Series securities, whereby one part of the government pays interest to another. There are no actual investments earning interest.

Social Security is unnecessary. A working American pays 12.4% of his salary[142] into Social Security - a large percentage of income allocated to a program that, according to the Social Security Administration itself, "was never intended to be your only source of income when you retire."[143] Social Security also provides disability benefits. Disability insurance is already available through the private market and/or as an employee benefit in many companies.

I propose we phase out Social Security. We should continue to pay benefits for those 65 years of age and older, and make no changes for those who are 60-64. For Americans between the ages of 40-59, we should raise the minimum age before one can receive benefits (which is currently set at 62). For Americans under the age of 40 (I, the author, am under 40), social Security benefits should be eliminated. However, all working Americans will need to continue paying Social Security taxes to pay for existing beneficiaries. Young people, for the foreseeable future, are simply going to have to pay for past generations' mistakes and poor decisions.

Does this sound extreme or uncaring? I don't think so. In the last year, I have spoken to many people my age and younger. I have not found one person who is planning on Social Security to be part of their retirement.

3. Phase out Medicare and Medicaid

As with Social Security, Medicare needs to be slowly phased out. The actual federal debt liability of this program ($38 trillion as of the end of FY2009, reviewed in Chapter 4) far exceeds even Social Security. Again, we need to implement a plan that will prepare younger Americans to assume responsibility for their own health care needs as they reach the age of retirement.

Medicaid should be rapidly eliminated at the federal level. Medicaid cost over $250 billion in FY2009, a 131% increase from 10 years prior. In addition to federal dollars, Medicaid is also paid via state funding, consuming on average over 20% of state annual budgets[144]. The States' ability to run up debt, however, is far more limited than the federal government. So let us say we did nothing more than push the entire burden of Medicaid to individual states. Each state would eventually be forced to develop cost effective programs. Right now, none of the states have opted out of Medicaid because of the funding they receive from the federal government. But the federal government is completely broke. A broke, debt-ridden individual doesn't pay for his relatives' health care; neither should our federal government.

4.   Eliminate public health care

The federal government should never have taken a role in health care for the elderly and/or poor. Health care is not a right. A discussion of how to "fix" health care in America is beyond the scope of this book, but let me suggest we already have the best healthcare system in the world. Be very suspicious of so-called world health care "ratings" from organizations whose primary goal is promoting free healthcare for everyone.[145]

The enormous debts of Medicare and Medicaid speak for themselves. Do we really want the federal government to take on a greater role in health care? As discussed in Chapter 7, the healthcare reform bill (ACA) of 2010 will cost at least $2-3 trillion in its first decade. This is likely a conservative estimate. Steve Hayward and Erik Peterson commented on the initial estimates of Medicare in 1993,

> *At its start, in 1966, Medicare cost $3 billion. The House Ways and Means Committee estimated that Medicare would cost only about $ 12 billion by 1990 (a figure that included an allowance for inflation). This was a supposedly "conservative" estimate. But in 1990 Medicare actually cost $98 billion.*[146]

Is there a socialized/communistic health care system in another part of the world we want to emulate? Public health care will result in higher costs[147] and poorer health care for everyone.

5.   Eliminate Federal Education and minimize Income Security Spending

In FY2010, the federal government spent approximately $108 billion on education. We can safely eliminate approximately $108 billion of this spending and be no worse off as a country. For one, the constitution does not grant the federal government the right to regulate or fund elementary or secondary education. Education, until the 1970's, was funded and run at the state level. Secondly, most of the Department of Education is unnecessary. Case in point – when the federal government shut down in November 1995 over a budget crisis, 89% of these employees were deemed nonessential and sent home[148]. Finally, student performance has not benefited from the federal government according to test scores[149].

Food stamps. Government housing. Supplemental security. Have welfare programs helped or harmed the vast majority of recipients? Federal spending on these programs needs to be drastically reduced (nearly $200 billion spent in FY2010). In the 1990's, we actually took a step in the right direction by reducing welfare. For an excellent analysis of welfare, before and after the Welfare Reform Act of 1996, I encourage you to read "The Effects of Welfare Reform" from the Heritage Foundation[150]. This article, written in 2001, identified the Welfare Reform Act's positive results in terms of reducing dependence and child poverty, while at the same time encouraging marriage. Unfortunately, recent legislation in 2009 has effectively reversed the 1996 reform act, ensuring a larger and worse off group of future dependents[151]. This is absolutely the wrong approach.

6. Eliminate Government Sponsored Entities (GSEs)

A GSE is defined as a "Privately held corporation with public purposes created by the U.S. Congress to reduce the cost of capital for certain borrowing sectors of the economy. Members of these sectors include students, farmers and homeowners."[152]

I mentioned two GSEs in Chapter 4 with respect to the housing market (Fannie Mae and Freddie Mac). The government describes these GSEs as follows:

> The housing GSEs (Fannie Mae, Freddie Mac, and the Federal Home Loan Bank System) are chartered by the Federal Government and pursue a federally mandated mission to support housing finance. Some GSEs are distinctly established as corporate entities - owned by shareholders of stock traded on the New York Stock Exchange. The obligations of the housing GSEs are not guaranteed by the Federal Government, however, Treasury's actions under HERA provided significant financial support to the GSEs.[153]

Let me provide a more accurate definition of a GSE:

> GSEs are created by the Federal Government and pursue a federally mandated mission of entitlement lending through risky financing that the private market

would rightfully avoid. Some GSEs are established as corporate entities – allowing for the privatization of short-term profits, often among government cronies. The obligations of the GSEs are not guaranteed by the Federal Government; however, as these GSEs inevitably fail, the government steps in and assumes all losses at taxpayer's expense.

GSEs are entitlements in the form of social/economic engineering – an attempt to provide equality by redistributing capital from creditworthy to un-creditworthy recipients. As the housing crisis demonstrated, GSEs can bring down a market and even the entire economy. We simply cannot afford to privatize profits and publicize losses[154].

Sadly, the same government that caused the housing crisis[155] is now seeking to use it as a way to grab more control over the private market[156]. This is unacceptable. Entitlements are a disaster. Equal rights, not equal things. A home (and a higher education for that matter) is not a right.

7. Enforce mandatory budget surpluses

Pass a constitutional amendment requiring each fiscal budget to result in a forecasted surplus of at least 10% of outlays. All outlays (including what is currently considered "off-budget") should be included. The only exception to this amendment would be during a formal declaration of war by Congress. Marginal tax rates for individuals and corporations should be returned to levels at or lower than what they were during the end of Ronald Reagan's presidency. No new national sales taxes e.g., VAT, wealth, estate, etc. Force the government to live within its means – every year.

For the short to medium term, generating surpluses may be difficult given the current levels of spending. This is where the 650 million acres of government owned land, valued at over $2 trillion in land and oil/natural gas mineral rights alone (refer to Chapter 4) will come in handy. Instead of closing vast areas of land to exploration and development, the government needs to leverage this additional revenue stream. For example, the Grand Staircase-Escalante National Monument (1.9 million acres of land in Utah) was designated as a U.S. National Monument by President Clinton in 1996[157] through the authority of the Antiquities Act. Not lost on residents of Utah is the fact that this monument sits on top of the largest coal deposit in the United States. Now, instead of generation plants, coal mines, jobs, and meaningful steps towards energy independence, these resources are effectively locked. Unfortunately, more land grabs by the federal government were being considered in 2010 as well.[158]

Summary

Debt is the result of decisions. Wars and financial recessions may result in deficits, but over the long haul, the debt is the result of the government taking decisions away from the individual. Social engineering and stimulus spending harms the economy and runs up debt; redistributive and entitlement programs are even more destructive. Entitlement programs devalue the individual, create unhealthy dependencies, and are difficult to end. They are the leading cause of the United States debt and the downfall of other countries.

The United States paid off its obligations once before, and we can do it again. Financial freedom is possible if the federal government recognizes, respects, and promotes free market economics, personal freedoms, and personal responsibility. But, this will only happen when the majority of our citizens recognize, respect, and promote these values through elections. It won't be easy, but I think it is still possible for our country to pay off its debts.

Appendix – The Causes of the Great Depression

–

What caused the Great Depression? Who and/or what was responsible? How did it end? In school, the story I learned went something like this:

> During the Roaring 1920's, people became rich by investing in the stock market. But, investors over-speculated by buying on margin, and the market eventually crashed. Many people lost their jobs and all of their savings. President FDR's New Deal helped the nation recover and prosper again.

This account is consistent with today's encyclopedias and textbooks. Consider the World Book Encyclopedia[159], where author Robert Sobel identifies the major causes of the Great Depression:

- Farm depression of the 1920's. Sobel points out many farmers struggled financially during the 1920's, while businesses prospered; over 500 banks in agricultural areas failed during the late 1920's.
- Uneven distribution of income. Workers in coal, railroad, and textile industries "failed to share in the prosperity of the 1920's." They could not buy goods as fast "as industry produced them." Many had to buy on credit, and then were forced to reduce spending to avoid debts. This caused the money in circulation to drop, harming business.
- The stock market crash. Rising stock values encouraged people to speculate, "that is, buy stocks in hope of making large profits." Stock values dropped, leading to a panic and an eventual mass sell-off.

A Deepening Depression

The depression deepened, Sobel continues, due in part to the laissez-faire policies of President Herbert Hoover. President Hoover "believed that business, if left alone to operate without government supervision, would correct the economic conditions." Hoover wanted support to come from state/local governments, but those governments "did not have enough money" to help. Hoover's most successful anti-depression measure, the Reconstruction Finance Corporation government agency, provided "some relief by lending money to banks, railroads, and other large institutions whose failure would have made the depression even worse." But dissatisfied Americans, who felt Hoover did too little to fight the depression, elected Franklin D. Roosevelt (FDR) President in 1932.

Note – the idea that Hoover did too little can also be found in a classical education children's history book[160] we use at my home,

> In 1932, President Hoover…set up something called the "Reconstruction Finance Corporation." The RFC was like a bank…so they [banks, businesses] could keep going until times got a little better…The RFC was a good start, but it wasn't enough…[FDR] promised Americans that if he were elected president…he would give America a "New Deal" that would reverse the Great Depression.

Big Government to the Rescue?

Sobel states FDR "believed the federal government had the chief responsibility of fighting the depression." FDR passed a series of laws called the New Deal to:

1. Provide relief to the needy
2. Aid recovery by providing jobs and "encouraging business"
3. Reform business and government to prevent a future Great Depression

The government also "aided recovery by spending large sums of money" which gave business leaders "the confidence to also begin spending". The economy began to improve, and the New Deal renewed America's confidence in the government. Many Americans lost faith, however, in bankers and business executives, and "decided that the government – not business – had the responsibility to maintain the national economy."

The classical education history book concurs,

> FDR created so many programs with abbreviations…Americans said, "FDR is making alphabet soup for the USA!" FDR's alphabet soup put real soup into the bellies of millions of hungry Americans. And his "New Deal" would slowly bring the United States out of the Great Depression."

Myths of the Great Depression

I urge you to download and read in its entirety, the article "Great Myths of the Great Depression," by Lawrence W. Reed of the Mackinac Center for Public Policy.[161] It is free, surprisingly easy to read, and a bit frightening. Reed does an effective job of dispelling the myths concerning Herbert Hoover, FDR, and how/why the Depression ended (some of which I discussed and presented in Chapter 6 and 7). Let us focus on what really caused the Great Depression. Reed identifies two major factors:

1. Economic engineering. Government monetary and credit supply policy heated up the economy, not greedy investors. According to one study, the Federal Reserve System increased the money supply by more than 60% from 1921-1929[162]. Note - increasing the money and/or credit supply, in an attempt to stimulate the economy or as means of entitlements, is a common practice of government.

2. More economic engineering. As Reed points out, there is a close relationship between the money supply and the economy; when a government increases the money and/or credit supply, interest rates will at first fall; business will increase investments and the economy will grow. When this boom slows, the economy cools. The government may then respond by slowing/contracting the money supply to stave off possible inflation. This is exactly what happened in the late 1920's. The Fed increased the discount rate (the rate member banks are charged for loans) from 3.5 to 6 percent between January 1928 and August 1929. The money supply dropped by 30% over the next 3 years, fueled in part by aggressive selling of government securities by the central bank.

What about the causes identified by Sobel?

- Farm depression of the 1920's. A farm depression may have played a part in the Great Depression, but what caused the farm depression? How about economic engineering? Specifically, the Fordney-McCumber Tariff of 1922 raised tariffs on agricultural imports in an attempt to protect domestic farmers from potentially cheaper imports following WWI[163]. This resulted in retaliatory tariffs from other countries, which in turn hurt both the domestic and international economies. And what about the bank failures? Author Jim Powell, in his book *FDR's Folly: How Roosevelt and His New Deal Prolonged the Great Depression*, noted that in the 1930's "Almost all the failed banks were in states with unit banking laws."[164]   Unit banking laws prevented banks from opening new branches and thereby diversifying risks.

- Uneven distribution of income. This argument lacks logic and appeals to class envy. Poor people, who by definition had little money to begin with, hurt the economy by buying on credit – and then later by saving?   As previously discussed, the drop in money circulation was due to government policy, not frugal poor people.

- The stock market crash. The stock market crash was a reflection and a result of government policies, not a cause of the Great Depression.   Margin requirements (the percentage of stock purchases that needed to be in cash) were no lower in the late 1920's than in previous decades, dispelling the popular explanation of margin lending leading to frenzied speculation.   Margin requirements had actually begun to rise by the fall of 1928. Additionally, stocks in the Dow Jones Industrial Average sold for 19x earnings at their peak, nowhere near what most analysts would point to as inflated. For example, Google's PE ratio as of December 2010 is 24, having peaked at over 150 in 2004.[165]

Notes

All of these notes are available at the book's website (www.UnderstandingTheUSDebt.com) where you can click on any of the URL's to go directly to the source articles.

Introduction

[1] I give credit for my initial interest in the debt to radio/T.V. personality Sean Hannity, who spent months rallying against the spending of the U.S. government in 2009.

[2] James Kwak, "GDP Growth Rates for Beginners", The Baseline Scenario, April 30, 2009. http://baselinescenario.com/2009/04/30/gdp-growth-rates-for-beginners/

Chapter 1

[3] The first fiscal year for the U.S. Government started Jan. 1, 1789. Congress changed the beginning of the fiscal year from Jan. 1 to Jul. 1 in 1842, and finally from Jul. 1 to Oct. 1 in 1977 where it remains today.
www.treasurydirect.gov/govt/reports/pd/histdebt/histdebt_histo5.htm

[4] The US initially went into debt in 1791 by assuming the war debts of the Continental Congress. Alexander Hamilton played a key role in consolidating the debt from among the colonies.

[5] CPI defined - http://www.bls.gov/cpi/cpifaq.htm. CPI values from the BLS are available for 1913-present. CPI values for 1790-1912 were sourced from www.measuringworth.com

[6] Gross Domestic Product (GDP) defined - http://en.wikipedia.org/wiki/Gross_domestic_product

[7] The Bureau of Economic Analysis (BEA) publishes GDP data for the U.S. economy - http://www.bea.gov/national/nipaweb/Index.asp. GDP values for 1790-1928 were sources from www.measuringworth.com

[8] Take a look at this reprint from the Maine Farmer issue, Deb 1834, talking about the extinction of the National Debt.
http://www.rootsweb.ancestry.com/~meandrhs/history/usdebt/1834.html

[9] "Economists point to rising debt as next crisis, Higher taxes and reduced federal benefits, services may be result", Associated Press, July 4, 2009. www.cnbc.com/id/31736145

[10] Martin Kelly, "Top 10 Founding Fathers", About.com.
http://americanhistory.about.com/od/revolutionarywar/tp/foundingfathers.htm

[11] For a great analysis of the Founding Fathers' view of frugality and debt, I encourage you to read The Five Thousand Year Leap, 28 Great Ideas That Changed the World, by W. Cleon Skousen.

[12] Ibid. A online quote from a prior book edition is available at
http://www.nccsstore.com/5000-Year-Leap/productinfo/5000YL

[13] "Sears, Roebuck and Co.", Lehman Brothers Collection – Twentieth-Century Business Archives, Harvard Business School, August 1983.
www.library.hbs.edu/hc/lehman/chrono.html?company=sears_roebuck_and_co
[14] "Greek Riots Continue as Markets Plunge", PBS, May 7, 2010.
www.pbs.org/newshour/extra/video/blog/2010/05/greek_riots_continue_as_market.html

Chapter 2
[15] Monthly Statement of the Public Debt (MSPD), U.S. Department of the Treasury, Bureau of the Public Debt. http://www.treasurydirect.gov/govt/reports/pd/mspd/mspd.htm
[16] A Citizen's Guide to the 2009 Financial Report of the U.S. Government, U.S. Department of the Treasury, Financial Management Service (FMS). www.fms.treas.gov/fr/09frusg.html
[17] Definitions of terms are available in the Terms worksheet of the Monthly Statement of the Public Debt Excel workbook. For example, the Sept. 2010 MSPD workbook can be downloaded from www.treasurydirect.gov/govt/reports/pd/mspd/2010/opdm092010.xls.
[18] "Ownership of Federal Securities", FMS, Sept 2010.
www.fms.treas.gov/bulletin/b2010_4ofs.doc
[19] In 2009, there is also a large spike in the "Other investors" category, defined as individuals, government-sponsored enterprises (GSEs), brokers and dealers, bank personal trusts and estates, corporate and non-corporate businesses, and other investors.
[20] U.S. Treasury Department, Major Foreign Holders of U.S. Treasury Securities (Sept 2010) - http://www.treas.gov/tic/mfh.txt
[21] "Old-Age and Survivors Insurance Trust Fund", Social Security Online.
www.ssa.gov/OACT/ProgData/describeoasi.html
[22] "Ponzi Schemes", The New York Times.
http://topics.nytimes.com/topics/reference/timestopics/subjects/f/frauds_and_swindling/ponzi_schemes/index.html
[23] "Trust Fund FAQ", Social Security Online. *"Far from being "worthless IOUs," the investments held by the trust funds are backed by the full faith and credit of the U. S. Government. The government has always repaid Social Security, with interest. The special-issue securities are, therefore, just as safe as U.S. Savings Bonds or other financial instruments of the Federal government".*
www.ssa.gov/OACT/ProgData/fundFAQ.html
[24] Jerry Robinson, "Social Security goes bankrupt", WorldNetDaily, May 18, 2009.
www.wnd.com/index.php?fa=PAGE.view&pageId=98406
[25] "Social Security & Medicare Tax Rates", Social Security Online. The initial Social Security tax rate in 1937 was 1%. It was raised several times over the next several decades, reaching 7% by 1970. In 1990, it was raised to the present rate of 12.4%. Medicare is taxed at 2.9%.
www.ssa.gov/OACT/ProgData/taxRates.html
[26] "Frequently Asked Questions about the Public Debt", TreasuryDirect.
www.treasurydirect.gov/govt/resources/faq/faq_publicdebt.htm

Chapter 3

[27] "1992 - Barbara Jordan DNC Keynote Speech", Thought Theater.
www.thoughttheater.com/2008/08/1992_-_barbara_jordan_dnc_keynote_speech.php
[28] "Frequently Asked Questions about the Public Debt", TreasuryDirect.
www.treasurydirect.gov/govt/resources/faq/faq_publicdebt.htm
[29] Conn Carroll, "The Never Ending TARP Slush Fund", The Heritage Foundation, Oct. 21, 2009. http://blog.heritage.org/2009/10/21/the-never-ending-tarp-slush-fund/
[30] World War I was not the only cause of increased spending. During his presidency (1913-1921), President Wilson also dramatically increased civil and general government spending. See the "Historical Statistics of the United States", p.g 299, U.S. Bureau of the Census, 1949. www2.census.gov/prod2/statcomp/documents/HistoricalStatisticsoftheUnitedStates1789-1945.pdf
[31] Ibid.
[32] Daniel Gross, "Restore the Estate Tax!", Slate, July 21, 2010. www.slate.com/id/2261254. Brian Riedl, "Obama Budget Raises Taxes and Doubles the National Debt", The Heritage Foundation, March 9, 2010. www.heritage.org/Research/Reports/2010/03/Obama-Budget-Raises-Taxes-and-Doubles-the-National-Debt
[33] Arthur Laffer, "The Laffer Curve: Past, Present, and Future", The Heritage Foundation, June 1, 2004. www.heritage.org/Research/Reports/2004/06/The-Laffer-Curve-Past-Present-and-Future
[34]"Historical Statistics of the United States", U.S. Bureau of the Census, 1949. www2.census.gov/prod2/statcomp/documents/HistoricalStatisticsoftheUnitedStates1789-1945.pdf
[35] "Outlays By Function", FMS, FY2009.
http://fms.treas.gov/annualreport/cs2009/outlay.pdf
[36] "10-Year Treasury Constant Maturity Rate", Board of Governors of the Federal Reserve System, January 04, 2011. http://research.stlouisfed.org/fred2/data/GS10.txt
[37] Ibid.
[38] "Veterans Services", U.S. Department of Veterans Affairs.
www.va.gov/landing2_vetsrv.htm
[39] I plan to post this what-if analysis scenario, in the form of a PowerPivot workbook, to the book's website.
[40] "1901-1932: The Income Tax Arrives", Tax History Museum.
http://www.taxanalysts.com/museum/1901-1932.htm
[41] Jim Powell, "No-So-Great Depression", National Review, January 7, 2009.
http://www.cato.org/pub_display.php?pub_id=9880
[42] Ed Rubenstein, "Introduction, the Real Reagan Record," National Review, August 31, 1992. http://old.nationalreview.com/reagan/intro200406101334.asp
[43] "Employment status of the civilian noninstitutional population 16 years and over, 1970 to date", U.S. Bureau of Labor Statistics, November 2010.
ftp://ftp.bls.gov/pub/suppl/empsit.cpseea1.txt

[44] "Bond Yields and Interest Rates: 1900 to 2002", U.S. Census Bureau, http://www.census.gov/statab/hist/02HS0039.xls

[45] Patrick J. Garrity, "Reagan and the Cold War", Ashbrook Center for Public Affairs, December 2002. www.ashbrook.org/publicat/onprin/v10n6/garrity.html

[46] David Asman, "Watch Out, More Government 'Stimulus' is Coming ", Fox Business, August 13, 2010. www.foxbusiness.com/markets/2010/08/13/watch-government-stimulus-coming/

Chapter 4

[47] Financial Report of the United States Government, FMS, www.fms.treas.gov/fr/index.html

[48] An additional guide to understanding the financial report is also available from "Understanding the Primary Components of the Annual Financial Report of the United States Government", Government Accountability Office, September 2005. http://www.gao.gov/new.items/d05958sp.pdf. -

[49] Page iv in the Citizen's Guide section of the Financial Report provides a brief summary of the difference between accrual and cash-based accounting. Annual budgets (and resulting deficits) are cash-based.

[50] "Accrual Based Accounting", MoneyInstructor.com. http://www.moneyinstructor.com/doc/accrualbased.asp

[51] Alec Aramanda, "The Public Student Loan Option", The Heritage Foundation, January 27, 2010. http://blog.heritage.org/2010/01/27/the-public-student-loan-option/

[52] Richard W. Rahn, "Where is the Balance Sheet?", The Washington Times, April 21, 2005. www.washingtontimes.com/news/2005/apr/20/20050420-085929-9595r/

[53] Michael J. Boskin, Marc S. Robinson, Terrance O'Reilly, Praveen Kumar, "New Estimates of the Value of Federal Mineral Rights and Land", National Bureau of Economic Research, May 1986, www.nber.org/papers/w1447

[54] David Walker, "Long-Term Fiscal Outlook: Action Is Needed to Avoid the Possibility of a Serious Economic Disruption in the Future," testimony before the [Senate Budget] Committee on the Budget, Jan. 29, 2008. http://gao.gov/new.items/d08411t.pdf

[55] Ibid.

Chapter 5

[56] "A Summary Of The 2010 Annual Reports Social Security and Medicare Boards of Trustees", Social Security Online, 2010. http://www.ssa.gov/OACT/TRSUM/index.html

[57] Ibid.

[58] The GAO summary (which includes this quote) can be found on pg. 27 of the FY2010 Financial Report. This statement also made recent headlines on FoxNews -

www.foxnews.com/politics/2010/12/23/gao-gives-auditing-government-medicare-projections-cites-uncertainties/

[59] "Budget of the United States Government: Citizen's Guide to the Federal Budget, Fiscal Year 2002.", GPO Access, 2002. http://www.gpoaccess.gov/usbudget/citizensguide.html

[60] Budget and Accounting Act, 1921, GAOUnion. http://gaounion.net/wp-content/uploads/2008/05/1921-budget-and-accounting-act.pdf

[61] "The Congressional Budget Process: An Explanation", United States Senate, December 1998. http://budget.senate.gov/democratic/commhist.html

[62] Ibid.

[63] CBO Fact Sheet, Congressional Budget Office, http://www.cbo.gov/aboutcbo/factsheet.cfm

[64] "A Guide to the FY 2011 Budget Process", the Concord Coalition, April 12, 2010. www.concordcoalition.org/publications/2010/0412/guide-fy-2011-budget-process

[65] Budget contents and submission to Congress, Cornell University Law School, http://www.law.cornell.edu/uscode/html/uscode31/usc_sec_31_00001105----000-.html

[66] The Budget, Office of Management and Budget, http://www.whitehouse.gov/omb/budget/Overview

[67] Postal Service outlays/revenues are also "off-budget", but are a fraction of Social Security outlays/revenues.

[68] Robert Longley, "The President's Budget Proposal, The First Step in the U.S. Federal Budget Process.", About.com, http://usgovinfo.about.com/od/federalbudgetprocess/a/budget_page1.htm

[69] Cliff Isenberg, "Congressional Leaders Make it Official: No Budget Resolution for FY2011", The Concord Coalition, June 28, 2010. www.concordcoalition.org/tabulation/congressional-leaders-make-it-official-no-budget-resolution-fy-2011

[70] Ibid.

[71] Congress's Fiscal Year 2011 Budget. Committee on the Budget, U.S. House of Representatives, 2010. http://budget.house.gov/singlepages.aspx?NewsID=1799

[72] "The Congressional Budget Process: An Explanation", United States Senate, December 1998. http://budget.senate.gov/democratic/the_budget_process.pdf

[73] Committee On Appropriations, United States House of Representatives, http://appropriations.house.gov/

[74] Senate Budget Committee, About the Committee, Glossary of Budget Terms, United States Senate. http://budget.senate.gov/democratic/glossary.html

[75] A Mid-Session Review for FY2011 can be found here - http://www.gpoaccess.gov/usbudget/fy11/pdf/11msr.pdf

[76] Robert Longley, "The Budget Reconciliation Process, What it is and is Not", About.com http://usgovinfo.about.com/od/uscongress/a/reconciliation.htm

Chapter 6

[77] Graeme Wearden, "Greece debt crisis: timeline", Guardian.co.uk, May 5, 2010, http://www.guardian.co.uk/business/2010/may/05/greece-debt-crisis-timeline

[78] The World Fact Book, Greece, U.S. Central Intelligence Agency, 2010. https://www.cia.gov/library/publications/the-world-factbook/geos/gr.html

[79] Carla Fried, "Greece Debt Crisis Puts Focus on Retirement Age", CBS Money Watch, March 1, 2010. http://moneywatch.bnet.com/retirement-planning/blog/retirement-beat/greece-debt-crisis-puts-focus-on-retirement-age/396/

[80] My research for Argentina came from several sources, which I have chosen to summarize in one endnote:
-The World Book Encylopedia, 1995.
-Wikipedia,
http://en.wikipedia.org/wiki/Economy_of_Argentina,
http://en.wikipedia.org/wiki/History_of_Argentina (The Radicals in Power, 1916-1930)
http://en.wikipedia.org/wiki/Radical_Civic_Union,
http://en.wikipedia.org/wiki/Juan_Per%C3%B3n,
http://en.wikipedia.org/wiki/Rogelio_Frigerio
-The World Fact Book, Argentina, U.S. Central Intelligence Agency, 2010. https://www.cia.gov/library/publications/the-world-factbook/geos/ar.html

[81] The historical summary of Japan was taken from the 1995 World Book Encyclopedia.

[82] Management techniques of W. Edwards Deming - http://web.dcp.ufl.edu/hinze/Deming.htm

[83] The World Fact Book, Japan, U.S. Central Intelligence Agency, 2010. https://www.cia.gov/library/publications/the-world-factbook/geos/ja.html

[84] World Economic Outlook (WEO) database, International Monetary Fund, October 2010. http://www.imf.org/external/pubs/ft/weo/2010/02/weodata/index.aspx

[85] Reiji Yoshida, "Bubble prophet fears new disaster". The Japan Times, Friday March 19, 2010. http://search.japantimes.co.jp/cgi-bin/nn20100319f1.html

[86] Ibid.

[87] Ibid.

[88] Bill Zielinski, "Japan' Solution To Debt Crisis - Expand Zombie Banking", Mortgaged Future, October 6, 2009. http://mortgagedfuture.com/japan-solution-to-debt-crisis-expand-zombie-banking/. For another very good set of graphs comparing the Japanese Housing Market of the 1990's to the U.S. Market of the late 2000's, see here - http://seattlebubble.com/blog/2008/11/03/comparing-the-us-and-japanese-housing-bubbles/

[89] Ronald Utt, Ph.D., "Lessons on How NOT to Stimulate the Economy", The Heritage Foundation, October 22, 2001. http://www.heritage.org/Research/Reports/2001/10/Lessons-on-How-NOT-to-Stimulate-the-Economy

[90] Anil K Kashyap, "Zombie Lending in Japan, How Bankrupt Firms Stifle Economic Reform", Capital Ideas, Sept. 2006. http://www.chicagobooth.edu/capideas/sep06/3.aspx

[91] Bill Zielinski, "Japan' Solution To Debt Crisis - Expand Zombie Banking", Mortgaged Future, October 6, 2009. http://mortgagedfuture.com/japan-solution-to-debt-crisis-expand-zombie-banking/

[92] Charles Smith, "Japan's Runaway Debt Train", Of Two Minds, 2001. http://www.oftwominds.com/japan.html

[93] Alan Reynolds, "Toward Meaningful Tax Reform in Japan.", Cato Institute, April 1998. http://www.cato.org/pub_display.php?pub_id=10982

[94] Ibid.

[95] Ibid.

[96] Brian Riedl, "Why Government Spending Does Not Stimulate Economic Growth: Answering the Critics ", The Heritage Foundation, January 5, 2010. http://www.heritage.org/Research/Reports/2010/01/Why-Government-Spending-Does-Not-Stimulate-Economic-Growth-Answering-the-Critics

[97] "Economic Stimulus Package," CCH Tax Briefing, CCHgroup.com, Feb. 13, 2008, http://tax.cchgroup.com/legislation/2008-stimulus-package.pdf

[98] "Summary of the 'Housing and Economic Recovery Act [HERA] of 2008", United States Senate Committee on Banking, Housing and Urban Affairs, June 17, 2008. http://dodd.senate.gov/multimedia/2008/072308_Housing.pdf

[99] S.896: Helping Families Save Their Homes Act of 2009, GovTrack.us, May, 2009. http://www.govtrack.us/congress/bill.xpd?bill=s111-896&tab=summary. The TARP Program is also summarized in the 2009 Financial Report of the United States Government (p.g. 13).

[100] Martin Fackler, "Japan's Big-Works Stimulus Is Lesson", The New York Times, February 5, 2009. http://www.nytimes.com/2009/02/06/world/asia/06japan.html

[101] "Dems power stimulus bill through Congress: Passage of $787 billion legislation hands Obama a critical political victory", Associated Press, February 14, 2009. http://www.msnbc.msn.com/id/29179041/

[102] Summary of Fiscal Year 2010 Budget Results, U.S. Treasury. http://www.ustreas.gov/press/releases/tg911.htm

[103] John H. Rogers, Ping Wang, "High Inflation: Causes and Consequences", Federal Reserve Bank of Dallas, Fourth Quarter 1993 Economic Review, http://www.dallasfed.org/research/er/1993/er9304c.pdf

[104] Martin Fackler, "Japan's Big-Works Stimulus Is Lesson", The New York Times, February 5, 2009. http://www.nytimes.com/2009/02/06/world/asia/06japan.html

[105] Meg Sullivan, "FDR's policies prolonged Depression by 7 years, UCLA economists calculate", UCLA Newsroom, August 10, 2004. http://newsroom.ucla.edu/portal/ucla/FDR-s-Policies-Prolonged-Depression-5409.aspx

Chapter 7

[106] As noted in the Chapter 1 graphs, event start and end dates were sourced from Wikipedia, which in turn summarized data from the National Bureau of Economic Research, www.nber.org

[107] Budget of the U.S. Government, Fiscal Year 2011, The Budget Message of the President (pg 1). www.gpoaccess.gov/usbudget/fy11/index.html

[108] "The role of Government Affordable Housing Policy in Creating the Global Financial Crisis of 2008, Staff Report, U.S. House of Representatives", 111th Congress. Committee on Oversight and Government Reform, July 7, 2009 http://blog.heritage.org/wp-content/uploads/2009/07/7-7-09-housing-crisis-report.pdf

[109] Mark R. Levin, Liberty and Tyranny – A Conservative Manifesto, (THRESHOLD EDITIONS; 1ST. EDITION edition), 2009

[110] Patrick Gibbons, "Old Myths about the New Deal", Nevada Policy Research Institute, Nov 4, 2008, www.npri.org/publications/old-myths-about-the-new-deal

[111] "Bush says sacrificed free-market principles to save economy", BreitBart, Dec. 15, 2008. www.breitbart.com/article.php?id=081216215816.8g97981o&show_article=1

[112] "Bush signs landmark Medicare bill into law", CNN, Dec. 08, 2003. http://articles.cnn.com/2003-12-08/politics/elec04.medicare_1_prescription-drug-private-insurers-medicare?_s=PM:ALLPOLITICS

[113] Derek Hunter, "Medicare Drug Cost Estimates: What Congress Know Now", The Heritage Foundation, April 28, 2005. http://www.heritage.org/Research/Reports/2005/04/Medicare-Drug-Cost-Estimates-What-Congress-Knows-Now

[114] "Inaugural Speech of Franklin Delano Roosevelt, Given in Washington, D.C. March 4th, 1933", History and Politics out Loud. http://www.hpol.org/fdr/inaug/

[115] All of the information about FDR in this section (as well as the information about Hoover in the preceding section) was taken from Reed's article – see Appendix

[116] Overview of funding, U.S. Government Recovery website, Dec. 04, 2010. www.Recovery.gov

[117] Michael D. Shear, "Obama Lesson: 'Shovel Ready' Not So Ready", The Caucus, Oct 15, 2010, http://thecaucus.blogs.nytimes.com/2010/10/15/obama-lesson-shovel-ready-not-so-ready/

[118] Jeffrey H. Anderson, "CBO: Obamacare Would Cost Over $2 trillion," Weekly Standard, Mar 18, 2010. www.weeklystandard.com/blogs/cbo-obamacare-would-cost-over-2-trillion

[119] James Sherk, "Majority of Union Members Now Work for the Government", The Heritage Foundation, Jan 22, 2010, www.heritage.org/Research/Reports/2010/01/Majority-of-Union-Members-Now-Work-for-the-Government

[120] Amanda Ruggeri, "Obama Plan to Grant TSA Workers More Union Rights Renews Debate Over Security Effect", U.S. News, Nov 20, 2008, http://politics.usnews.com/news/national/articles/2008/11/20/obama-plan-to-grant-tsa-workers-more-union-rights-renews-debate-over-security-effect.html

[121] Carl Horowitz, "Obama Arranges Takeover of GM and Chrysler; Auto Workers Union Gets Huge Stake", National Legal and Policy Center, May 01, 2009, http://www.nlpc.org/stories/2009/05/01/obama-administration-arranges-takeover-gm-and-chrysler-auto-workers-union-gets-hu

[122] Ibid.

[123] Rep. Steve Scalise (LA), "Cap and Trade Will Cost American Families ", GOP.gov (originally posted on Townhall.com), April 23, 2009, http://www.gop.gov/blog/09/04/23/cap-and-trade-will-cost

[124] "CBO: Cap-And-Trade to Cost $175 Per Household", Environmental Leader, June 23, 2009, http://www.environmentalleader.com/2009/06/23/cbo-cap-and-trade-to-cost-175-per-household/

[125] $1300 amount cited by Peter Orszag (OMB Director), Rep. Steve Scalise (LA), "Cap and Trade Will Cost American Families ", GOP.gov (originally posted on Townhall.com), April 23, 2009, http://www.gop.gov/blog/09/04/23/cap-and-trade-will-cost

[126] "Incomplete CBO Estimate Does Not Include All Costs of Cap-and-Trade", United States Senate Republican Party Committee, July 8th, 2009, http://rpc.senate.gov/public/_files/EnergyFactsCBOScore.pdf

[127] Ibid.

[128] Ben Lieberman, "The Waxman--Markey Global Warming Bill: Is the Economic Pain Justified by the Environmental Gain?", Heritage Foundation, Junes 23, 2009, www.heritage.org/Research/Testimony/The-Waxman-Markey-Global-Warming-Bill-Is-the-Economic-Pain-Justified-by-the-Environmental-Gain

[129] Ibid.

[130] Sheldon Filger, "Federal Reserve Begins Massive Monetization of U.S. Government Debt", Huffington Post, August 11, 2010. www.huffingtonpost.com/sheldon-filger/federal-reserve-begins-ma_b_677483.html

[131] Ray Kurzweill, The Age of Spiritual Machines Glossary, http://www.kurzweilai.net/the-age-of-spiritual-machines-glossary. Knee of the Curve: the period in which the exponential nature of the curve of time begins to explode. Exponential growth lingers with no apparent growth for a long period of time and then appears to erupt suddenly. This is now occurring in the capability of computers.

[132] "2010 Election Winners", Bloomberg Business Week, http://www.businessweek.com/magazine/2010-election-results/

[133] "The Tea Party Movement Principles", Tea Party Patriots, http://teapartypatriots.org/BlogPostView.aspx?id=af49c010-5dab-4fca-8c06-921181d52b37

Chapter 8

[134] I originally came across the statistic that over half of the world lives on less than $2 a day in the book Crazy Love by Francis Chan. www.crazylovebook.com

[135] "More Than Half the World Lives on Less Than $2 a Day", The Population Reference Bureau, 2005.
http://www.prb.org/Journalists/PressReleases/2005/MoreThanHalftheWorldLivesonLess Than2aDayAugust2005.aspx

[136] U.S. Census Bureau Poverty Threshold 2005, one person under 65 years (Note – I divided the annual value of $10160 by 365 to get $27.83.), U.S. Census Bureau, 2005. www.census.gov/hhes/www/poverty/data/threshld/thresh05.html

[137] Table B-1, Income, Poverty, and Health Insurance Coverage in the United States: 2005, U.S. Census Bureau, 2005. http://www.census.gov/prod/2006pubs/p60-231.pdf

[138] This list is virtually identical to what W. Cleon Skousen identified in his book The Five Thousand Year Leap, 28 Great Ideas That Changed the World.

[139] 1 Timothy 5:8, ESV Bible,
http://www.gnpcb.org/esv/search/?passage=1+Timothy+5%3A8

[140] "FDR's Statements on Social Security", Social Security Online.
http://www.ssa.gov/history/fdrstmts.html

[141] William Beach and Gareth Davis, "Social Security's Rate of Return", The Heritage Foundation, January 15, 1998. http://www.heritage.org/Research/Reports/1998/01/Social-Securitys-Rate-of-Return. Be sure to also review the follow up article that responds to criticisms of their first article -
http://www.heritage.org/Research/Reports/1998/12/Calculating-Social-Securitys-Rate-of-Return

[142] 6.2% of an employee's salary (up to $106,800 in 2010) is allocated to Social Security; employers match this amount. Those who are self-employed pay the entire 12.4%. http://www.socialsecurity.gov/pubs/10003.html

[143] Your Social Security Statement (Feb 25, 2010), pg 1. Also available online - http://www.ssa.gov/pubs/10006.html.

[144] "State Expenditure Report Fiscal Year 2008", National Association of State Budget Officers - www.nasbo.org/Publications/StateExpenditureReport/tabid/79/Default.aspx

[145] The world health report 2010 – Health systems financing: the path to universal coverage, World Health Organization, www.who.int/whr/en/

[146] Steven Hayward and Erik Peterson, "The Medicare Monster,", Reason.com, January 1993. http://reason.com/archives/1993/01/01/the-medicare-monster

[147] John Goodman, "Health Reform Will Make Health Insurance More Expensive for Individuals", National Center For Policy Analysis, Dec. 1, 2009. www.john-goodman-blog.com/health-reform-will-make-health-insurance-more-expensive-for-individuals/
http://www.heritage.org/research/reports/2009/11/union-contracts-of-health-care-workers-would-inflate-health-care-costs

[148] John Blankenship, "Department of Education influence should be limited", The Register-Herald.com, November 5, 2010. www.register-herald.com/columns/x1364885021/Department-of-Education-influence-should-be-limited

[149] Ibid.

[150] Robert Rector, "The Effects of Welfare Reform", The Heritage Foundation, March 15, 2001. www.heritage.org/Research/Testimony/The-Effects-of-Welfare-Reform

[151] Mike White, "President Obama Ends Welfare Reform", Associated Content, March 6, 2009. www.associatedcontent.com/article/1525977/president_obama_ends_welfare_reform.html

[152] "Government-Sponsored Enterprise - GSE ", Investopedia, http://www.investopedia.com/terms/g/gse.asp

[153] 2009 Financial Report of the United States Government, p.g. 16, www.fms.treas.gov/fr/09frusg.html

[154] "The role of Government Affordable Housing Policy in Creating the Global Financial Crisis of 2008, Staff Report", U.S. House of Representatives, 111th Congress. Committee on Oversight and Government Reform, July 7, 2009 http://blog.heritage.org/wp-content/uploads/2009/07/7-7-09-housing-crisis-report.pdf

[155] Ibid.

[156] Jane Sasseen, "Obama Presses for Financial Reform", Business Week Sept. 2009. http://www.businessweek.com/bwdaily/dnflash/content/sep2009/db20090914_694458.htm

[157] "Grand Staircase-Escalante National Monument", New World Encyclopedia, www.newworldencyclopedia.org/entry/Grand_Staircase-Escalante_National_Monument

[158] Michelle Malkin, "Obama's Land Deal Power Grab", FrontPageMag.com, Aug. 16, 2010, http://frontpagemag.com/2010/08/16/obamas-land-deal-power-grab/

Appendix

[159] The World Book Encylopedia, 1995.

[160] Susan Wise Bauer, the Story of the World, History for the Classical Child, Volume 4: The Modern Age, (Revised edition, 2005).

Note – in defense of this book series, I find them in general to be well written and entertaining, even for an adult! However, the accurate and insightful study of history is a key tenant of classical education. Bauer's coverage of the Great Depression needs improvement.

[161] Lawrence W. Reed, "Great Myths of the Great Depression,", Mackinac Center for Public Policy, Sept 2005, www.mackinac.org/archives/1998/sp1998-01.pdf

[162] Ibid.

[163] Edward S. Kaplan, "The Fordney-McCumber Tariff of 1922", EH.net, Feb 2010, http://eh.net/encyclopedia/article/Kaplan.Fordney

[164] Jim Powell, FDR's Folly: How Roosevelt and His New Deal Prolonged the Great Depression, (New York: Crown Forum, 2003), p. 32.

[165] Google PE Ratio, YCharts, http://ycharts.com/companies/GOOG/pe_ratio

9728870R0

Made in the USA
Lexington, KY
23 May 2011